The QuickBooks Cookbook™ Guide to...

Online Banking, Transaction Downloading, and Online Bill Payment in QuickBooks®

By Mark Wilsdorf

Published by

FLAGSHIP TECHNOLOGIES, INC.

MADISON, MISSOURI, USA

www.goflagship.com

Online Banking, Transaction Downloading, and Online Bill Payment in QuickBooks

First edition

PUBLISHER

Flagship Technologies, Inc.
14976 Monroe Road 1039
Madison, MO 65263

www.goflagship.com

> *This book is dedicated to QuickBooks Professional Advisors, CPAs, and the local "bookkeeper down the street" in your community: people who have made it a part of their life's work to help you achieve success with QuickBooks as your most important small business accounting tool.*

Table of Contents

CHAPTER 1

Introduction

The title of this book pretty much describes everything that it is about: using online banking, transaction downloading, and online bill payment services from within QuickBooks. An exceptionally narrow focus, you say? Well, you may find that this book's focus is *even more narrow* than the title implies, because it spends a lot of time on the *mechanics* of using online financial services—the step-by-step procedures you need for getting various jobs done in Quick-Books.

Why write a book with such a narrow focus? Here are some of the reasons/needs/situations this book was written to address:

◆ **Many long-time QuickBooks users** are just now venturing into using online financial services. If that describes you, you may be seeking advice and perspectives on how online banking, etc. relate to the QuickBooks tasks you already do, and to your daily workflow.

◆ **Even if you are experienced with "the QuickBooks way of doing things"** you may feel unsure about what electronic transactions are or how to use them in QuickBooks. Or you may be hesitant about what steps to take to begin downloading transactions from your bank or credit card company. But you don't likely need a 600-page "everything-but-the-kitchen-sink" QuickBooks reference. You probably just need a few bits of information to help you get started—a brief discussion of the "whats" and "whys" related to using online financial services, and some step-by-step instructions for common tasks.

◆ **If you are new to QuickBooks** you have a lot of things to learn, and it probably seems that you need to learn all of them *yesterday!* So right now you may only be interested in learning the basics—how to enter income and expense transactions, add Customers and Vendors, print a balance sheet, etc.—knowing that you can learn other aspects of using QuickBooks later as your time and needs allow. When the time comes for adding online financial services to your repertoire of QuickBooks skills, you can pick up this book for a quick introduction to the subject, regardless of how much time has passed since you began using QuickBooks.

◆ **If you've searched the Web for free tutorials and information** about using online financial services in QuickBooks, you have probably found that some of it is good...and some of it is not. But just as big a problem, is that it is scattered across literally thousands of Web pages, blog articles, and forum message posts. You can spend *hours* browsing the Web to find the pieces of information you need—often gathered from several different Web sites. By contrast, this book is meant to be a cohesive, one-stop shop for that information.

About this Book

Who it is written "to"

This book is written to you, with the assumption that you are someone directly responsible for keeping the accounting records of a small business, using QuickBooks. If that's not quite correct I'll at least assume you have an interest in the management of, or accounting for, a small business, and that you want to know how using online financial services will affect your daily QuickBooks accounting processes and workflow.

Its examples and screenshots are from *desktop* editions of QuickBooks

Trying to cover too many bases with any book is a recipe for disaster; or at least, for mediocrity and limited usefulness. This book *could* have been written to cover using online financial services in both QuickBooks Online and the desktop versions of QuickBooks. But the extra screenshots, comments, slightly-different procedures, and so on, would have made it overly complicated—maybe even downright confusing—in some places. And that would have made it less useful to at least part of its target audience.

Consequently, all of the procedures, screenshots, and information in this book are based on *desktop* editions of QuickBooks; specifically, on QuickBooks 2013 for Windows. Which edition? ...Pro, Premier, or Enterprise? That doesn't really matter. The online banking features of all three are essentially identical, so everything in this book applies equally to all of them.

So does all this mean that this book has no value for QuickBooks Online users? On the contrary! The approaches and procedures for setting up and using online financial services are similar in all QuickBooks accounting software products. So if you use Quick-Books Online you'll find that this book is a pretty good fit for you as well. Mainly, the appearance of your screens will be different from the screenshots shown in this book even though they will contain identical information in most cases. Otherwise, the information and procedures you need are nearly identical to what you will find here.

It's a bit redundant...a bit redundant ...a bit redundant

You'll notice that some topics and procedural steps are duplicated in a few places. The goal is to give you everything you need to know about a particular topic in one place, without asking you to jump around to different parts of the book. While this makes for a bit of redundancy it avoids breaking the "flow" of information, making it easier to follow the steps in a procedure without loosing your place.

An apology to all of my past English teachers...

I apologize in advance if the grammar and punctuational styles used in this book offend you. Intentionally written to be informal and conversational, it bends the rules of grammar a bit here and there in hopes of making it comfortable to read.

A few of you (Mrs. Haggard? Mr. Duvall? Mr. Kropf?) may want to blame me for single-handedly setting in motion the demise of the English language. But I hope you will exercise some restraint—please, no bricks thrown through my living room window. I would also remind you that frustrating situations beyond our control are just a part of life up with which we must all put.☺

I only hope you won't try to revoke any of my diplomas. (Uh...you can't really do that, can you?)

Errors? Comments? ...Email me!

In any book that contains a lot of technical information, there are plenty of opportunities for error. If you find errors—especially ones which could lead other readers to incorrect results or conclusions—I hope you'll contact me by email at Flagship Technologies, Inc. My direct email address there is mrw@goflagship.com, and I welcome all comments, criticisms, and suggestions related to this book.

However, please don't email me asking for individual help with your QuickBooks-related questions or problems. Instead, post them in one of Flagship Technologies' online forums at www.goflagship.

com/forums/, or one of the many other QuickBooks message forums on the Web, such as 🌐 community.intuit.com.

The "Ground Rules"

The following text styles and symbols are used through this book to convey special meaning:

Vendors > Pay Bills	Indicates a series of menu selections. This example means to select Vendors from the main menu, then Pay Bills from its submenu. (The ">" character is included just to separate the individual selections.)
Ctrl-R	Indicates a key or keys to be pressed. This example means to press the "R" key while holding down the "Ctrl" (Control) key.
🌐 goflagship.com	Links or Web addresses marked with a small "earth" graphic link to a Web page.
Show hints	This type style is used when describing text in a window or dialog in QuickBooks or another program.
7	Print versions of this book display references to other pages as a small page symbol containing a page number.
★	Informational note.
🔧	Technical note—often about QuickBooks settings, etc.
▲	Warning or cautionary note.
	Sidebar technical notes and comments.
💡	Sidebar hints, tips, and ideas.

CHAPTER 2

About Online Financial Services in QuickBooks

About this chapter	This chapter lays the groundwork for the rest of the book by describing the essential ideas, workflow/procedures, and management considerations for using online banking and related financial services in QuickBooks.

Online Financial Services Basics

Problem I know QuickBooks can do online banking—paying bills and transferring funds between accounts electronically, online. But I've also heard that QuickBooks can download my credit card transactions, even if I don't use other online banking features. That ought to save me the effort of typing them in manually —and that really interests me. Is online banking easy to do? Will downloading transactions really save me any time?

Solution Online banking and downloading credit card transactions are both fairly easy to learn and use. While they can save time in many cases, that's not always so. A lot depends on when you choose to make entries in QuickBooks, and the kinds of entries you make most often.

Discussion Probably the biggest factor in deciding whether or not you will use QuickBooks' online banking features is personal preference. Some people are resistant to using them because of the changes in accounting habits they require, or security concerns, or for other reasons.

While your bank and credit card company may offer various online financial services, the path to using them in QuickBooks is not completely lined with roses. There are minor difficulties to deal with, new techniques to learn, and strategies to figure out for getting the most out of online services without creating more problems than they solve.

Aside from these considerations, the bottom line is this: you need to think of online financial services as being no different from a smartphone, or GPS, or barcodes, or any other technology you use in your business. There are costs and benefits associated with it, and your job is to figure out whether the benefits outweigh the costs in *your* situation.

The purpose of this section is not to provide detailed steps for using online financial services—those will come later. Rather, it is meant to give you an overview of online services as they relate to Quick-Books, and to explore some of the problems and opportunities involved, as well as potential costs and benefits.

Before we get started, here are some definitions you will need:

◆ **Electronic transaction:** A transaction which transfers funds between accounts or between people or businesses without using physical checks, deposits, or other paper documents. Many electronic transactions accomplish their fund transfers using ACH transactions, but alternative services like MasterCard's RPPS network are increasingly used also.

 ACH (Automated Clearing House) transactions are electronic transactions which banks use for transferring funds to and from other banks via the Federal Reserve system. When you give someone a check and they deposit it, an ACH transaction is what transfers funds from your account in your bank to the payee's account in his or her bank.

In QuickBooks, electronic transactions are often referred to as "online transactions". That does not mean they are necessarily entered online (on a Web page); in many cases, they are entered in QuickBooks and are merely *processed* online, when you send/receive transactions to/from your bank or credit card company (or a third-party bill payment service).

Electronic transactions are most often used for **online banking** and **online bill payment** purposes, to send payments to other people or businesses, including payments to the bank or credit card company.

⭐ You <u>do not</u> have to use electronic transactions to benefit from using online financial services in QuickBooks! For instance, many people download credit card transactions into QuickBooks to save data entry time and effort, without ever entering any electronic transactions.

◆ **Online banking:** Using QuickBooks and an Internet connection to access details of your bank account (current balance, most recent bank statement, etc.), download transactions which have cleared the account (checks and deposits), and in some cases, to transfer funds between accounts or make payments to the bank electronically—such as making a loan payment without having to send a physical (paper) check.

◆ **Online bill payment:** Paying amounts owed to other people or companies by sending an electronic transaction to your bank or to an online bill payment service. The electronic transaction describes who to pay, when (on what date) to make payment, and the payment amount. Your bank or bill payment service will deduct the payment from your bank account and transfer it to the payee's account, usually via an ACH transaction. If the payee cannot receive an electronic transaction, the bill payment service may mail them a physical (printed) check.

◆ **Transaction downloading:** Using an Internet connection to retrieve transactions (checks and deposits, or credit card charges and payments) which have cleared a bank account or a credit card account. You can import downloaded transactions into Quick-Books as a way to add new transaction entries without typing them in manually.

How Online Transaction Processing Works

Working with bank accounts, credit card accounts, and online bill payment differs in minor ways, but the steps involved are basically the same. The sections below provide a brief overview of the steps involved for various activities.

Set up an online connection for an account

This is something you do one time, for each bank or credit card account you want to be able to access online.

On the financial institution's Web site,
**register for online access to your
bank account or credit card account,**
getting a user ID and password to use
in the next step.

In QuickBooks, **set up an online connection** **for the desired account** (a bank or credit
credit card account in the QuickBooks Chart
of Accounts), supplying the online user ID
and password from the prior step so that
QuickBooks can connect to and access the
account to send/receive transactions.

Enter electronic transactions in QuickBooks (optional)

Electronic transactions are a way to send payments to others
through the banking system, rather than using printed checks. Note
that many people download bank or credit card transactions
(discussed later in this section) without ever choosing to use
electronic transactions.

Enter an electronic transaction **in
QuickBooks,** usually on the Pay Bills,
Write Checks, or Transfer Funds forms.
Be sure to check the required box to have
the transaction processed electronically.

*(Electronic transactions you have entered
are stored for processing later when
you send/receive transactions.)*

Send/receive transactions in QuickBooks

Some people refer to this step as "synchronizing" the bank or credit
card account with QuickBooks.

Open the Online Banking Center
(Banking > Online Banking >
Online Banking Center).

Select the financial institution and account(s) you want to synchronize, then click Send/ Receive Transactions 30 . QuickBooks sends any electronic transactions you have entered and retrieves (downloads) any transactions which have cleared the account since your most recent send/receive.

(Downloaded transactions are not entered directly in QuickBooks. They are stored in the Online Banking Center, and can be added to QuickBooks later if you want, as described in the next topic.)

Add downloaded transactions to QuickBooks (optional)

This may be the most popular online banking feature, because of the typing effort it can save. Transactions downloaded in the send/ receive step, described above, are compared with existing Quick-Books transactions. Any downloaded transactions which match an existing transaction are not added to QuickBooks—because that would result in duplicate transactions. Any downloaded transactions which *do not* have a match are available for you to complete (by filling in any missing or optional information) and add to QuickBooks.

Open the Online Banking Center
(Banking > Online Banking > Online Banking Center).

Click Add Transactions to QuickBooks 35 .

(QuickBooks compares the transaction amounts, dates, and payee names of downloaded and existing transactions, determining which ones match.)

11

For each *Unmatched* **transaction** 39 (ones which don't match any of your existing transactions), you may...

Select a vendor name for the
unmatched transaction.

Select an account for the
unmatched transaction.

Click the Add Transaction button
to add the downloaded transaction to
QuickBooks as a new transaction entry.

Online Financial Services: Things to Know Before You Begin

Does my bank or my credit card company support online access?

Before you can get started with online banking or downloading credit card transactions, you need to find out whether your bank or credit card company offers online access. Also, find out what *level* of online services they make available.

Most banks and credit card companies offer at least "informational" online services: they let you access your account balance, transaction history, and monthly statements through their Web site (after registering on the site, so that your account information can be accessed securely). That kind of access is usually free as part of the company's standard customer service offerings and does not involve a monthly fee.

But just viewing account information online is not the same as downloading transactions to QuickBooks, or transferring funds between accounts electronically, or paying bills online. Your bank or credit card company may provide some or all of those services, for free or for a monthly fee.

Online bill payment services are available from two sources:

1. Your bank (though many banks don't yet offer online bill payment), or

2. A third-party bill payment service provider.

Intuit (the maker of QuickBooks) is one of those third-party providers. Their QuickBooks Bill Pay Service (www.quickbooks.intuit.com/product/ add_ons/bill_pay.jsp) is competitively priced and offers good QuickBooks integration. Intuit markets the service through Web page links in QuickBooks: clicking a link takes you to directly to the service's Web site, making it easy to sign up.

Other providers offer similar services, some with even more advanced QuickBooks integration than Intuit's service. www.Bill.com is one of these: it offers comprehensive bill payment services and excellent QuickBooks integration.

To find out whether your financial institution supports exchanging transactions with QuickBooks you can call and ask them. But you can also find out by checking within QuickBooks:

1. **Open the Participating Financial Institutions window** (Banking > Online Banking > Participating Financial Institutions).

2. **Click on the type of online access you are interested in,** such as *Banking account access*, in the upper left pane.

3. **Scroll through the list in the lower part of the left pane** to see if your financial institution is listed there.

4. **Click on the institution's name in the left pane** to display the kinds of online services it supports, in the right pane.

 The Participating Financial Institutions window lists all of the banks, credit card companies, and online payment services which currently support exchanging transactions with QuickBooks.

A financial institution must register with Intuit to be included in this list. If you do not see your bank or credit card company listed there, contact them to ask whether they support downloading to QuickBooks. They may be in the list but listed under a slightly different business name than you expect.

What does it cost?

Online banking plans which allow **downloading bank transactions** to QuickBooks often range from $0 (free) to around $15 monthly. The fee is often higher for the more automated direct connection 21 downloading method, and lower (free in most cases) if you are willing to get transactions by downloading and importing Web Connect files 21.

Most credit card companies which support downloading let you **download credit card transactions** for free.

Online bill payment fees range from $0 (free) to $25 or more per month

14

(usually depending on transaction volume) and may involve a per-transaction fee in some cases. Bill payment services also typically charge an additional $1 or more for printing and mailing a physical check, when a payee cannot accept electronic payments.

Fees toward the lower end of the range are typical among banks, where online bill payment may be considered as just one of a range of benefits offered to customers. Third-party services like ❂ www. Bill.com tend to cost more but may offer a wider range of services and better QuickBooks integration.

What are the benefits?

Here are some potential benefits of using online financial services. Many of these are discussed in greater detail later in this section.

◆ **Time savings.** Downloading transactions instead of entering them manually may save time if done carefully and correctly. Otherwise, you may spend more time fixing errors than you save by downloading transactions.

◆ **Reduced costs for postage, paper, and supplies.** Online bill payment avoids all of the costs associated with mailing payments: the cost of pre-printed check forms and envelopes, printer ink or toner cartridges, postage, and so on.

Some savings are available even if you don't use a full online bill payment service. Most banks let you transfer account balances online; say, from a savings or money market account to your checking account. And most credit card companies let you make payments on your credit card balance using electronic transactions to transfer funds from your bank.

◆ **More timely payments; fewer late payment charges.** Online bill payment services and many credit card companies let you "calendarize" payments. You schedule the dates on which payments are to be made, and they will be made automatically on those dates—with no further intervention from you. This can prevent late payment fees and finance charges caused by forgetting to make a payment or by not mailing a payment far enough ahead of its due date.

◆ **Lower fees charged by your accountant?** Even if you have no interest in downloading bank or credit card transactions on your own, if someone else does your bookkeeping it may speed up data entry for them and reduce the fees they charge. For example, if you hire a local accounting firm to enter checks and deposits and reconcile your bank and credit card balances every

month, giving them online access to your accounts for downloading transactions will likely save them time. Most accountants charge by the hour for such services, so that should
reduce the fees you will pay.

 What about security for your online accounts? Giving your accountant online access to bank and credit card accounts is at least a minor
security risk. You simply have to decide whether you trust the people at
your accounting firm enough to give them that kind of access.

But think about this: Employees of your *bank* have access to your bank
account, and employees of your *credit card company* have access to
your credit card account—and you probably don't know any of those
people personally. People at a local accounting firm pose no greater
risk, especially if the firm has good policies in place for protecting your
online account information. Just be sure to ask how they protect the
privacy of sensitive data before you provide it to them.

What about data security? Is my information safe if I access it online?

That's a good question, for which there isn't a definite answer.

Accessing your account online, or downloading transactions, or
paying bills online involves *very little* added security risk. Financial
data is sent and received over a secure (encrypted) Internet connection, which makes it nearly impossible for the data stream to
and from your financial institution to be unscrambled and
"harvested" for illegal use.

Data is almost never stolen from the brief online connections that
occur between a computer and a bank or credit card company. For
information thieves, the real prize is getting access to *thousands* of
accounts. They are much more likely to be interested in hacking
into your credit card company's data storage system where thousands of records are kept, than in the meager prospect of harvesting
your individual data from an Internet connection—especially given
the tremendous technical difficulty of getting that done (the
sophisticated encryption methods used are a major hurdle).

Here's the point: accessing your own financial data online does not
make it any less secure than it already is. The encrypted connections used for that kind of data access are quite good at keeping
your data protected while it is being transmitted to/from your
financial institution. The point of greatest risk is where your data is
stored by your bank or credit card company, and protection from
that risk is entirely out of your hands—you have no control over it,
except to switch to a different bank or credit card company. Security

for your personal identity and financial account information depends mostly on the security systems in place at your bank or credit card company, *regardless of whether you choose to access it online or not.*

 An exception to all of this is if your computer is infected with a virus or malware designed to harvest data as you type at the keyboard—known as a "key logger". These can harvest account and PIN numbers as you type them, such as when you log in to your bank's Web site.

The best defense against malware and viruses is to be sure you are running recommended security software on your computer—a firewall and an anti-virus/anti-malware program, at least—and that you keep User Account Control (UAC) turned on. (UAC is a feature of Windows Vista and later, including Windows 7 and Windows 8.)

Aren't paper transactions more secure than electronic transactions?

Paper transactions are often <u>less</u> secure! With old-style paper credit card forms—you know, where an imprint of your card is transferred onto a multi-part carbon form—your credit card information is more vulnerable to theft through careless handling and disposal of the paper forms. Stealing credit card information from paper forms in a dumpster or trash can was common when card-imprint machines were in wide use.

What do I need to know about my edition of QuickBooks being "sunsetted" by Intuit?

If you use a desktop edition of QuickBooks, you probably know that Intuit "sunsets" each annual QuickBooks edition, usually after about three years of availability and support. For instance, if you use QuickBooks 2013 you can expect it to be sunsetted by about 2016 unless Intuit changes its sunsetting schedule.

What does "sunsetting" mean? In general, it means that Intuit stops providing technical support, program updates, and other services for that QuickBooks edition. It *does not* mean your copy of Quick-Books will stop working! It only means that Intuit will stop supporting it.

Why is this important if I use online financial services? One of the kinds of support Intuit drops when it sunsets an edition is access to all online services, including online financial services. In other words, that edition will no longer be able to use online banking and related features—transaction downloading, sending online payments, electronic transfers between accounts, etc.

What's the solution? Generally, you'll have to upgrade to a newer version of QuickBooks if you want to continue using online financial services—something to consider as an added cost if you otherwise would not have chosen to upgrade your copy of QuickBooks so soon.

> ⭐ **An alternative to upgrading** is to purchase a third-party QuickBooks add-on which can import Web Connect files [21] into your current QuickBooks edition. Going this route will require you to manually download the Web Connect files from your bank or credit card company's Web site. Given the extra effort required, most users opt for upgrading to a newer edition of QuickBooks.

Does sunsetting affect QuickBooks Online (QBOL)? No. Online versions of QuickBooks are always current and are never "sunsetted" as the desktop editions are. (Unlike the desktop editions though, using QBOL requires paying a monthly subscription fee.)

What kinds of transactions "make sense" to download? Which are most likely to save me time and effort if I capture them by downloading?

You need to consider whether you work with enough of the kinds of transactions which yield benefits from being captured by downloading, to justify the effort (and sometimes, cost) involved.

Bank accounts

◆ **Deposits** should always be entered in QuickBooks before you send them to the bank. You should *never* intentionally capture them by downloading except in rare cases.

Why? Because a downloaded deposit transaction contains sparse details about the individual checks or cash amounts that were included in the deposit. That makes it difficult to know which account(s) should be credited with income or which customer invoices were paid. Also, if you don't have a detailed record of your deposits you cannot know which ones are still outstanding (have not yet cleared the bank) or even whether one may have been lost in the mail—rare, but it does happen. So you cannot know your current bank balance with certainty, and cannot correctly reconcile the account.

◆ **Checks you will print from QuickBooks** obviously have to be *entered* in QuickBooks before you can print them. So when you download transactions from the bank those check entries will already exist in QuickBooks. When QuickBooks compares downloaded and existing transactions it will see those check entries as matching and will not add them (to avoid adding duplicate transactions). In short, no data entry effort will have been saved by downloading these check transactions.

◆ **Handwritten checks** are a different story. They may or may not have been entered in QuickBooks prior to downloading transactions. So you might benefit from capturing them by downloading rather than entering them manually—but with one warning: it is important to know which handwritten checks are still outstanding (have not yet cleared the bank). If you don't know that, you cannot know your correct bank balance including outstanding items.

If you decide to allow handwritten check transactions to be captured by downloading rather than entering them manually, be sure to at least keep track of the checks you've handwritten during the month—a paper checkbook register or checkbook stubs works fine for this. After downloading transactions from the bank, manually enter any checks that were not included in the download (because they had not yet cleared the bank). That way, when you reconcile you'll know the correct bank balance including outstanding items.

◆ Like handwritten checks, **debit card transactions** (purchases and refunds) don't necessarily have to be entered in QuickBooks before they clear the bank. Also, debit cards are often used for small-amount purchases. Together, these two facts make debit card transactions good candidates for capturing by downloading. So long as your bank account has an adequate balance to cover them, you might capture debit card transactions every couple weeks or even at the end of the month, prior to reconciling the bank account.

Debit card transactions are also like handwritten checks in that some may still be outstanding when you download transactions. To properly reconcile your bank account then, you need to have a record of debit card purchases during the month. Keeping an envelope or pouch of debit card purchase receipts is one way to do that. Before reconciling the account you can manually enter any debit card transactions which have not yet cleared the bank, so that reconciling the account will provide you with the correct bank balance including outstanding debit card purchases.

The bottom line: In a typical small business you may already have entered most **checks and deposits** manually by the time you download transactions from the bank. So if most of your transactions are checks and deposits, downloading bank transactions won't save you much time. But if you write a lot of **handwritten checks** or use a **debit**

card for many purchases, you probably *will* save time by downloading bank account transactions.

 Electronic checks are a different story. They are always entered manually—either in QuickBooks or on the Web site of your bill payment service—so that they can then be processed online. Either way, they should be present in QuickBooks before you download bank transactions. (If they were entered on a bill payment service's Web site, they get added to QuickBooks when you synchronize with the Web site.)

Downloading only captures what has *cleared* the bank!

In case it is not obvious from this discussion, it bears repeating that downloaded bank transactions only include checks, deposits, and debit card transactions which have *cleared* the bank.

The only way you can know your true bank balance is to be sure that *all* checks and debit card purchases—including ones which have not yet cleared the bank—have been entered in QuickBooks. And the only way you can get that done is by having some sort of record of them. For handwritten checks that may be a check register. For debit card purchases it more often will be an envelope, pouch, or folder containing the month's paper receipts.

Credit card accounts

◆ **Credit card charges** are a good candidate for capturing by downloading, because they don't normally have to be entered in QuickBooks at any particular time—they only need to be there before reconciling the credit card account. If the credit limit on your card is high enough that you are not concerned about exceeding it during the month, you might just download credit card transactions once a month—right before reconciling the account.

◆ **Credit card payments** (payments on the credit card balance) are normally entered in QuickBooks when you make payment on the account, and that is usually done by writing a check or using an electronic transaction. This means they should already be present in QuickBooks when you download transactions, resulting in no time savings for downloading them.

The bottom line: Most QuickBooks users *will* save time and effort by downloading credit card transactions.

Two ways to connect

QuickBooks supports two methods for connecting to your bank or credit card account, and your financial institution may support either of them, or both:

◆ **Direct Connect.** QuickBooks connects directly to the financial institution's server computer, over an Internet connection. This connection is two-way, allowing QuickBooks to both send and receive transactions. So it supports sending (uploading) electronic transactions you have entered in QuickBooks, as well as receiving (downloading) transactions which have cleared your account, so that you can add them to QuickBooks.

◆ **Web Connect (file download).** With this method your financial institution makes a file available for downloading from their Web site, containing transactions which have cleared your account— usually for a range of dates you choose. You download the file by clicking a link on their Web site, then import the file (file name extension .QBO) into QuickBooks (Banking > Online Banking > Import Web Connect File). This connection method is one-way: it only supports *downloading* bank or credit card transactions for adding to QuickBooks, not sending (uploading) electronic transactions that you have entered.

The Direct Connect method is the more automatic of the two. Using Web Connect isn't difficult, but it may require that you remember the location (i.e., hard drive folder) where you saved the Web Connect file when you downloaded it, so that you can locate the file for importing into QuickBooks.

You can find out which connection method(s) your financial institution supports by opening the Participating Financial Institutions window (Banking > Online Banking > Participating Financial Institutions) and clicking on the institution's name in the left pane of the window, as described earlier 13.

When a financial institution is listed twice in the left pane that typically means it supports both connection methods. In the following example "DC" or "WC" appear following the bank name to indicate the two connection choices (Direct Connect and Web Connect, respectively). However, not all banks which support both connection methods are listed this way.

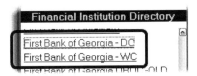

This page is intentionally blank.

Getting Started with Online Banking

Setting Up Online Connections for Your Accounts

Problem

I've checked with my bank and my credit card company, and both of them allow downloading transactions into Quick-Books. I'd like to give it a try...but how do I get started?

Solution

Establish an online account at your bank or credit card company first. Then use the features in QuickBooks to connect your QuickBooks financial accounts with their corresponding online account services.

Discussion

Establishing an online account at your bank or credit card company can be as simple as registering on their Web site (setting up a user ID and password) and supplying information to verify your identity as an account holder. You may also have to agree to pay a monthly fee if the financial institution charges one for online access.

Once you have a user ID and password for your online account, you can supply that information in QuickBooks to establish a connection between specific accounts in your Chart of Accounts—maybe your checking account, savings accounts, and/or credit card accounts—with their counterparts at the bank or credit card company.

QuickBooks stores the user ID and password information separately for each account connection. So later when you want to retrieve bank or credit card transactions, QuickBooks will be able to log in to your account automatically.

Bank / Credit Card Company Setup

At your bank or credit card company:

◆ **You must have an account** with the bank or credit card company before doing anything else.

If you are switching to a new bank or a different credit card, establish an account with the financial institution first, before setting up the account in QuickBooks.

◆ **Register for an online account** on the financial institution's Web site.

This will establish the user ID and password which you—and QuickBooks—will use for accessing account information and services online.

QuickBooks Setup

In QuickBooks, you will connect an account in your Chart of Accounts with its corresponding online services. Here's an example of setting up an online connection for a credit card account—the steps are the same for a bank account.

1. **Select** Banking > Online Banking > Set Up Account for Online Services.

   QuickBooks will open the Set Up Account for Online Services window.

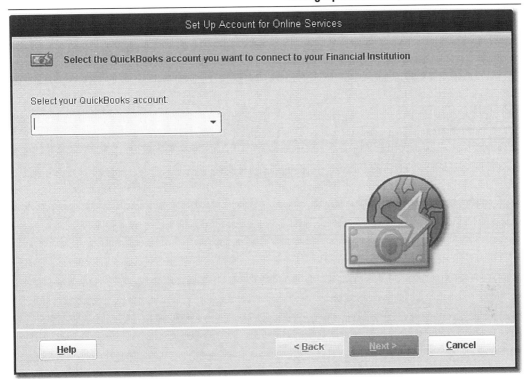

2. **Select the account** you want to connect to online services, **then click Next.**
   Or add a new account by clicking the down arrow and selecting <Add New> from the drop-down list, **then click Next.**

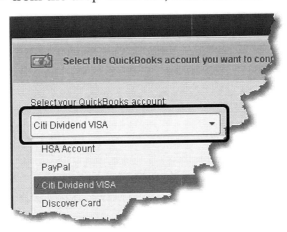

⭐ **Usually you will be selecting an existing account in this step.** But if you are opening a new bank account or have a new credit card and it does not yet exist in the QuickBooks Chart of Accounts, this step is where you should add it.

3. **Select the name of your bank or credit card company** from the drop-down list, **then click Next.**

The list is a long one, but you can speed up finding your financial institution by typing the first few letters of its name in the drop-down list box. That will scroll the list to the name's approximate location, where you can find and select it.

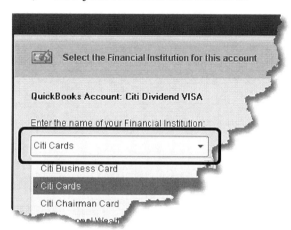

4. If QuickBooks asks, **choose the type of online connection you want to use, then click Next.**

If your financial institution supports both connection methods (described in chapter 2 | 20 |) QuickBooks will ask which connection method you want to use.

5. **Enter the login information** for your online account, **then click the Sign In button.**

This provides QuickBooks with what it needs for signing in to your account, so it can send and receive transactions.

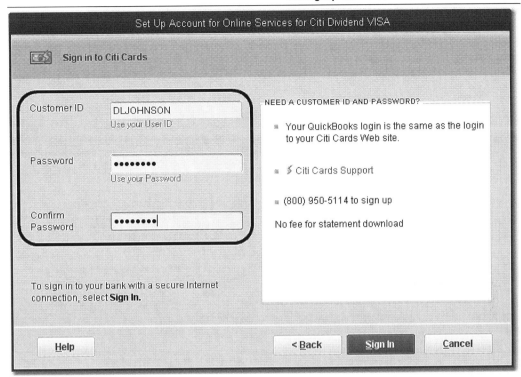

After you click the Sign In button, QuickBooks will log in to your online account and retrieve a list of the account(s) you hold at that financial institution (bank or credit card company). For instance, you might have both a checking account and a savings account at the same bank.

6. **Select the bank or credit card account** corresponding to the Quick-Books account you selected in step 2, **then click Next.**

If you only have one account at the financial institution, only one will be listed. In other cases such as for a bank where you have multiple accounts, each of them will be listed and available to select.

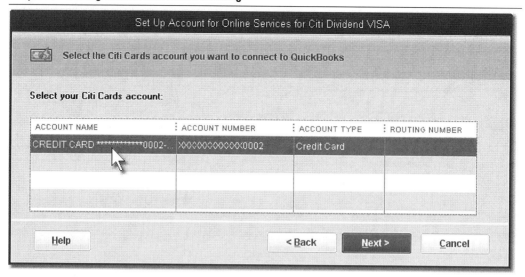

In this example, selecting the "CREDIT CARD ************0002" account tells QuickBooks that it corresponds to the account named "Citi Dividend VISA" in the QuickBooks Chart of Accounts.

After clicking Next, QuickBooks will tell you that you've completed setting up the connection.

7. **Click Finish** to close the Set Up Account for Online Services window.

If QuickBooks informed you that it had downloaded transactions (after step 6), next you'll be taken to the Online Banking Center where you can add the transactions to QuickBooks 35 or delete them 50 if desired. In the example below, only one transaction was downloaded during setup of the account's online connection.

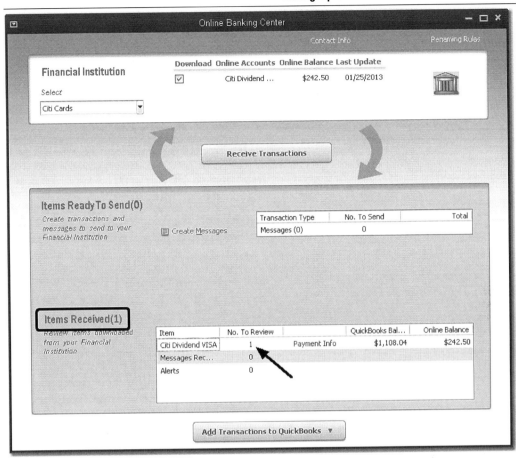

⭐ **If this is the first time you've downloaded transactions** for the account, it is possible that some old (already-reconciled) transactions were retrieved. For hints on how to handle them, see *The very first time you download, watch out for duplicates!* 53 in chapter 4.

Sending/Receiving Electronic Transactions

Problem I want to download transactions from my bank or credit card company, to get them into QuickBooks. How do I do that? And how can I send electronic transactions to my bank for processing?

Solution Use the Send/Receive Transactions feature in the Online Banking Center, to both upload (send) and download (receive) transactions from your bank or credit card company.

Discussion Some people refer to sending/receiving transactions as "synchronizing" with the bank or credit card account. Transactions which have cleared the account since your most recent send/receive will be downloaded, and any electronic transactions you have entered in QuickBooks (such as a transfer of funds from a savings account to your checking account) will be sent to the financial institution for processing.

It's worth noting here, that downloading (receiving) transactions _does not_ automatically add them to QuickBooks: you control which transactions get added, and when. The steps for adding transactions to QuickBooks will be discussed in chapter 4 ⌐35⌐.

How to Send/Receive Transactions (Direct Connect)

1. **Open the Online Banking Center** (Banking > Online Banking > Online Banking Center).

2. **Select the financial institution** you want to synchronize with.

   QuickBooks will update the Online Banking Center display with statistics for the financial institution you selected, including summaries of electronic transactions ready to send, the online balance from your most recent send/receive session, and other information, as the following illustration shows.

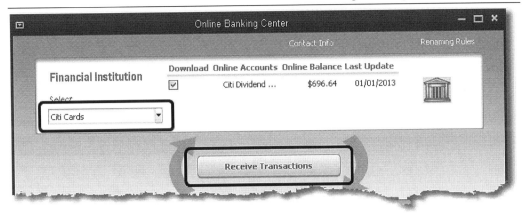

3. **Click the Receive Transactions button.** (It will be labeled Send/
   Receive Transactions if you have any pending electronic transactions to send.)

4. When prompted, **enter your PIN number or password** for the online
   account, **then click OK.**

   QuickBooks will then:

   ◆ Establish an Internet connection to the financial institution.

   ◆ Process any pending electronic transactions.

   ◆ Download transactions which have cleared the account since
   your most recent prior send/receive.

   ◆ Update the Online Banking Center display to show the
   account's online (cleared) balance and a summary of the
   downloaded transactions, as shown here:

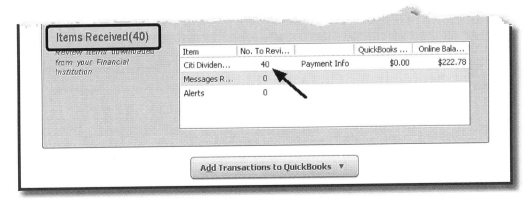

You can initiate sending/receiving transactions directly from several different QuickBooks forms and windows. Once you've established online access for an account, its Register window will have a button like this in the menu bar:

Likewise, forms where the account's transactions are entered will have a similar button:

Clicking either of these buttons will open the Online Banking Center and will pre-select the account (in this example, a credit card account), so that you can begin downloading transactions by simply clicking the Receive Transactions button there.

How to Receive Transactions (Web Connect file)

As mentioned earlier, downloading a Web Connect file is a one-way method for connecting to your bank or credit card account. That is, a Web Connect file supplies downloaded transactions but does not give you any way to send (upload) electronic transactions that you have entered in QuickBooks.

Though the details will differ a bit from one bank or credit card company to another, the general steps for downloading and importing a Web Connect file are the same:

1. **Start your Web browser** (Internet Explorer, Firefox, etc.), and **log in to your bank or credit card company's Web site.**

2. **Navigate to the Web page for downloading Web Connect files.**

At this point, some financial institutions will let you specify a date range for the transactions to download. Others will present a list of files available for downloading; often, each file will contain all transactions which cleared the account in a particular calendar month or statement period.

You may also be asked to choose the file's format. If so, choose Web Connect, or QuickBooks, or .QBO—any of these should result in downloading a QuickBooks Web Connect file.

3. **Click on the appropriate link** to download the Web Connect file to your computer.

   Your browser should display a dialog box asking whether you want to Open or Save the file.

   ◆ **If you select Open** the file will be downloaded, then automatically opened for importing into QuickBooks.

   ◆ **If you select Save** you'll be asked to choose a location (on your computer) for saving the file, which you'll need to remember so that you can import the file into QuickBooks later.

4. <u>If you selected Save</u>, **import the file into QuickBooks** by selecting Banking > Online Banking > Import Web Connect File.

   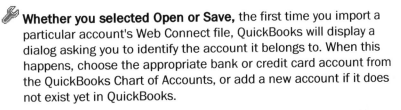 **Whether you selected Open or Save,** the first time you import a particular account's Web Connect file, QuickBooks will display a dialog asking you to identify the account it belongs to. When this happens, choose the appropriate bank or credit card account from the QuickBooks Chart of Accounts, or add a new account if it does not exist yet in QuickBooks.

   Finally, QuickBooks will import the file and show information about the downloaded transactions in the Items Received section of the Online Banking Center (Banking > Online Banking > Online Banking Center):

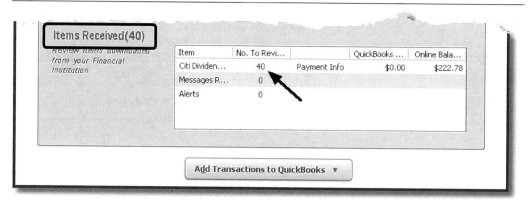

⭐ **Importing a Web Connect file** *does not* **mean you have imported its transactions into QuickBooks.** Imported transactions only go into the Online Banking Center; from there you must add them to QuickBooks⌐35⌐ as described in the next chapter.

CHAPTER 4

Adding Downloaded Transactions to QuickBooks

About this chapter	This chapter gets to the heart of the online banking feature of greatest benefit to the largest number of QuickBooks users: adding downloaded transactions to QuickBooks as transaction entries—and in the process, saving a lot of typing.

Adding Downloaded Transactions to QuickBooks

Problem

OK, I've downloaded (sent/received) transactions ⌐30⌐ and I see information about them in the Online Banking Center. But how do I bring the downloaded transactions into QuickBooks —so they show up in my QuickBooks registers and reports?

Solution

Use the Add Transactions to QuickBooks feature in the Online Banking Center.

Discussion

Adding downloaded transactions to QuickBooks is *not* like "dumping them in with a bucket"—you have full control over exactly which transactions get added, and when.

It is a process which (1) automatically matches downloaded transactions with ones you've already entered, to prevent adding duplicates, (2) lets you add or change the Vendor, Account, Class, etc. of any transaction before adding it, (3) lets you control which transactions are added, and (4) provides features that let you "teach" QuickBooks about the various way payee names are spelled in downloaded transactions, so that over time the downloading/ matching/adding process becomes more automated.

How to Add Downloaded Transactions to QuickBooks

Adding downloaded transactions to QuickBooks is simple to do, but the first time you do it the necessary steps aren't entirely apparent. To better explain each part of the process, it is broken down into separate sections below.

Opening the Add Transactions to QuickBooks Window

To get started you need to select a bank or credit card account to work with.

1. **Open the Online Banking Center** by selecting Banking > Online Banking > Online Banking Center.

   If QuickBooks asks you to choose an online banking mode, choose Side-by-Side Mode. (Register Mode can be a bit confusing when you're new to adding transactions.)

2. In the upper pane of the Online Banking Center window, **select the financial institution** for the transactions you want to add.

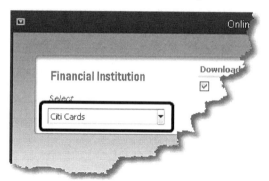

After selecting the financial institution in the upper pane, the lower pane will show how many transactions are available for adding to QuickBooks.

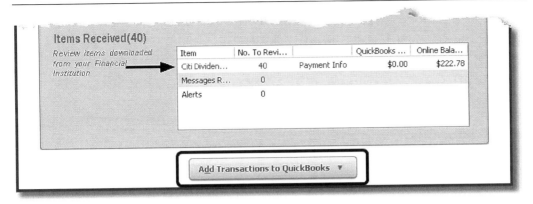

3. **Click the Add Transactions to QuickBooks button.**

QuickBooks will display a pop-up window listing your account(s) at this financial institution so that you may choose an account to work with.

4. **Click on the account you want to work with.**

The Add Transactions to QuickBooks window will then open, for the account you selected.

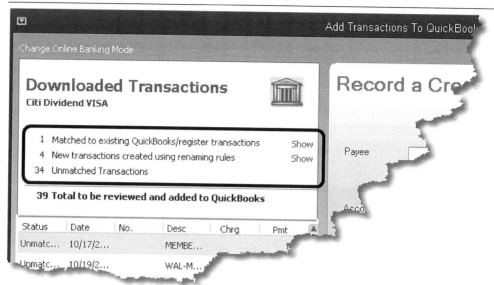

The upper left pane shows statistics about the available transactions:

◆ **Matched transactions** are downloaded transactions which match existing transactions (based on a comparison of payee/vendor name, amount, etc.) and which therefore won't be added to QuickBooks.

◆ **New transactions created using renaming rules** are transactions that were downloaded from your financial institution and which (1) don't match any existing transactions, but (2) can have a vendor name and account filled in automatically by QuickBooks, based on the renaming rules[55] you have created. These are transactions QuickBooks can add automatically if you wish, with no editing or other intervention by you.

◆ **Unmatched transactions** don't match any existing transactions and don't fit any of your renaming rules[55]. These are transactions you need to complete, by selecting a payee name and an account, before they can be added to QuickBooks.

After you've been importing transactions for several months, unmatched transactions will usually fall into either of two categories:

1. Transactions involving existing vendors (ones already in your Quick-Books Vendors list) but which either use a slightly different spelling of the vendor's name or have added numbers or other characters in the Payee field, preventinng QuickBooks from automatically linking them with an existing vendor name, or...

2. **Transactions involving new vendors**—people or businesses not yet added to your QuickBooks Vendors list.

The sections below tell how to work with each of these transaction categories.

Complete Unmatched Transactions

Credit card charge example

Charges against an account—whether a credit card charge, a check drawn on a bank account, or a withdrawal from a savings account—are all handled the same way:

1. **Click on the *Unmatched transactions* link** in the upper left pane of the Add Transactions to QuickBooks window[36].

   A list of unmatched transactions will be displayed in the lower left pane.

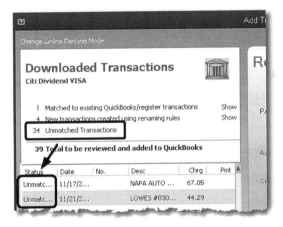

2. **Click on a transaction in the lower left pane**, to work with that transaction.

   The transaction's Payee and Amount fields will appear in the right pane, ready for you to fill in.

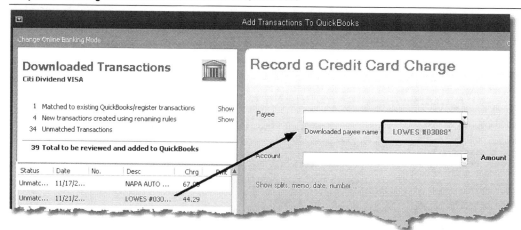

3. **Select a payee** in the Payee field.

   The Payee field may already be filled in if the payee name in the downloaded transaction exactly matches one of your QuickBooks names (a Vendor, Customer, etc.).

   In the example above, the Payee field is empty because the downloaded payee name ("LOWES #03088*") is not an *exact* match for any name in any QuickBooks name list. After selecting a Payee, the Payee field will look like this:

   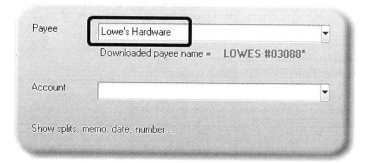

4. **Select an account** in the Account field.

   Selecting an account here is fine if the *entire* transaction amount should be posted to that account—for example, a purchase of fuel for one of your business' vehicles. But what if you need to split the transaction between two or more accounts? The next step shows how to do that.

5. **Click the *Show splits, memo, date, number...* link.**

The right pane changes to reveal a lot more detail about the transaction, including a section where you can select multiple accounts and amounts, to allow splitting the transaction several ways. (See the example below.)

6. **You can split the transaction if you want,** by selecting different accounts and amounts on each line and dividing the total amount among them, as shown here:

Record a Credit Card Charge

▶ More matching options

Date	11/21/2012
Number	
Payee	Lowe's Hardware
	Downloaded payee name = LOWES #03088"
Memo	**Amount**　　44.29

Expenses

Account	Amount	Memo	Customer:Job	Billable	Class
Repairs	17.43	Machinery bearing		☐	
Chemicals	26.86	Epoxy adhesive		☐	
				☐	

Remove Selected　　　　　　　　**Total Expenses: $44.29**

Hide splits, memo, date, number ...

Add to QuickBooks

7. When you are done editing the transaction, **click the Add to QuickBooks button.**

If you selected a Payee name in step 2, QuickBooks may display a message to notify you that it has created a new Renaming Rule. This just means that the next time QuickBooks sees a downloaded transaction with a payee name spelled as it was in this one, it will match that transaction with the same Vendor,

Customer, etc., as you selected here. (When QuickBooks applies renaming rules to your transactions, that is how they automatically get added to the *New transactions created using renaming rules* category described earlier in this chapter⌐38⌐.)

★ **See the renaming rules** ⌐55⌐ **discussion** in chapter 5 for more details on automatically matching payee names in downloaded transactions with your QuickBooks name lists.

8. **Repeat steps 2 through 7 for each of the Unmatched transactions.**

When you are done, only Matched and/or New transactions should remain to be added to QuickBooks, as shown in the upper left pane of the window.

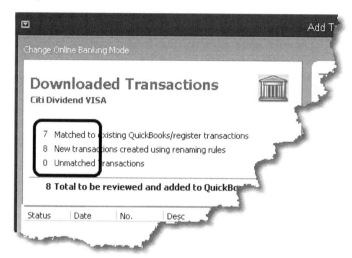

At this point you *could* click the Done (or Finish Later) button in the lower right part of the window, to immediately add the Matched and New transactions to QuickBooks. But usually it's best to review the New transactions before allowing QuickBooks to add them. Why? Because New transactions were created automatically by QuickBooks, based on your renaming rules⌐55⌐, and in some cases QuickBooks may have assigned *accounts other than what you intend* to those transactions.

Bank deposit example

Additions to an account—whether a deposit to a checking or savings account, or a payment or credit on a credit card account—are all handled similarly. The main goal is to be sure that income gets assigned to the correct income accounts. If you invoice customers, another goal is equally important: you need to ensure that customer payments included in a deposit get associated with the correct invoices so those invoices will be marked as paid in QuickBooks.

This example shows how to associate received payments with deposits "after-the-fact"—after the deposits have cleared the bank. As discussed in chapter 2 18 , this probably isn't a good practice. It omits outstanding deposits (ones that have not yet cleared the bank), so it means your bank balance in QuickBooks can never be assumed to be current. It can also lead to errors and confusion: it is simply too easy to associate payments with the wrong deposits.

However, this practice can be successful if handled properly:

1. Keep good handwritten details of every deposit—a detailed copy of a deposit slip will do—so that you can associate the right payments with your downloaded deposit entries before adding them to QuickBooks.

2. Download and add bank account transactions to QuickBooks often— while the details of recent deposits are fresh in your mind and easy to recall.

Here is an example of how to complete a downloaded deposit transaction, including associating customer payments with it.

1. **Click on the *Unmatched transactions* link** in the upper left pane of the Add Transactions to QuickBooks window 36 , to display a list of unmatched transactions in the lower left pane.

2. **Click on a deposit transaction in the lower left pane,** to work with that transaction.

   The transaction's details will appear in the right pane.

   ◆ If you have any amounts in Undeposited Funds or have any open invoices (ones your customers have not yet paid), the right pane will have tabs near the top for selecting those items to include in the deposit. (See the boxed area, below.)

   ◆ The lower part of the right pane (indicated by the arrow, in the screenshot below) allows entering income directly, to include in the deposit.

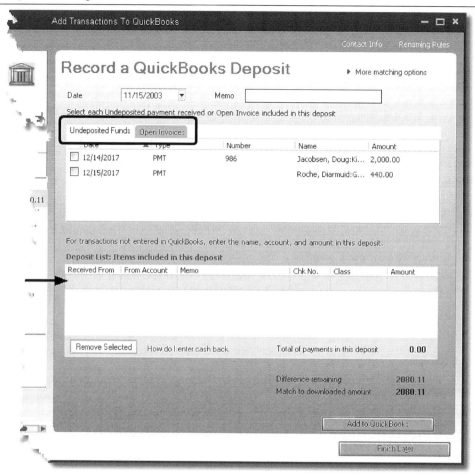

⭐ **The Undeposited Funds account** is a sort of "holding tank" for payments you have recorded in QuickBooks but have not yet deposited. Selecting payments from the Undeposited Funds tab in this window will remove them from Undeposited Funds and include them in the deposit entry.

⭐ **Open invoices** represent unpaid invoice amounts owed to you by your customers. Selecting invoices from the Open Invoices tab in this window will mark them as paid, and will include their amounts in the deposit—the assumption is that the deposit is recording receipt of full customer payment on those invoices.

3. **Select Undeposited Funds and/or open invoice amounts to include in the deposit** by check marking them on their respective tabs.

The following example shows an item on the Undeposited Funds tab, check marked to include in the deposit.

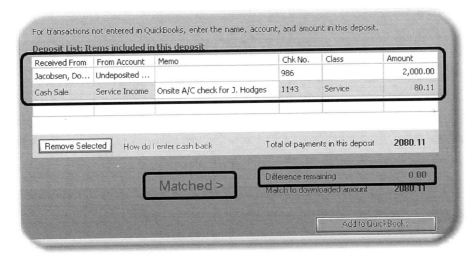

4. **Enter any other payments or income included in the deposit,** in the lower part of the right pane. Fill in the columns as desired.

   The first line in the example below shows the $2,000.00 Undeposited Funds item from step 3, and the second (highlighted) line shows a check that has been added to the deposit.

The *Difference remaining* item shows the difference between the deposit entry's amount and the downloaded transaction's amount. *You won't be allowed to add the transaction to Quick-Books until these two amounts match.* When they do, the word "Matched" appears, as shown in the screenshot above.

5. When you are done editing the transaction, **click the Add to QuickBooks button.**

What if the deposit includes a *partial payment* of an open invoice?

You have two options for recording a partial payment:

1. **The least error-prone approach** is to leave the Add Transactions to QuickBooks window, and use the Receive Payments window (Customers > Receive Payments) to record the received payment and send it to the Undeposited Funds account. Then return to the Add Transactions to QuickBooks window. When you do, the partial payment will appear on the Undeposited Funds tab, where you can select it to include in the deposit.

2. **The second approach** is easy but requires understanding how Quick-Books works "behind the scenes". In the lower part of the right pane, select the customer name in the Received From column, select Accounts Receivable in the From Account column, then complete the rest of the line as you wish, being sure to enter the payment amount in the Amount column. If you do this, QuickBooks will connect the partial payment with the customer's account.

Review "New transactions created using renaming rules"

If QuickBooks created any new transactions based on your renaming rules⌊55⌉, it is a good idea to review those transactions before allowing QuickBooks to add them.

1. **Click on the *Show* link** beside *New transactions created using renaming rules* in the upper left pane of the Add Transactions to QuickBooks window.

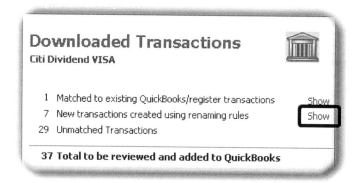

⭐ **The *Show* link** only appears if transactions are available to view.

The new transactions will be listed in the lower left pane, labeled with a status of "Renamed".

2. **Click on a transaction in the lower left pane**, to work with that transaction.

The transaction's details will appear in the right pane.

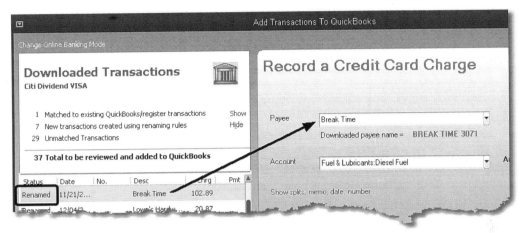

3. **Verify the transaction** by reviewing its details and making changes if necessary.

> Clicking the *Show splits, memo, date, number...* **link** will give you access to more transaction details, and will allow you to split the transaction among multiple accounts as described earlier 41 or to edit the Memo, assign a Class or Customer:Job, etc.

4. When you are done editing the transaction, **click the Add to Quick- Books button.**

QuickBooks will immediately add the transaction, removing it from the New transactions list.

5. **Repeat steps 2 through 4 for each of the New transactions.**

What about Matched transactions?

Generally it's not necessary to review them. They don't represent "new" transactions that will be added; but rather, transactions that *will not* be added because they match existing transactions (have the same dates, amounts, payees, etc.).

Finish (Confirm Matched and/or New Transactions)

When no unmatched transactions remain, and you have (optionally) reviewed new and/or matched transactions, you are ready to finish adding the downloaded transactions to QuickBooks.

1. **Click the Done button**—or the Finish Later button if you want to quit without processing all of the Unmatched transactions right now.

   If you have any Matched and/or New transactions, QuickBooks will ask if you want to add them.

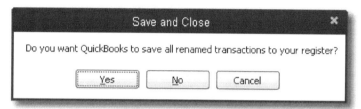

2. **Click Yes** to add New transactions to QuickBooks and confirm Matched transactions.

Adding Many Transactions at Once, Using the Add Multiple Feature

You can speed up adding transactions by using the Add Multiple feature.

1. **Open the Add Transactions to QuickBooks window,** as described earlier 36.

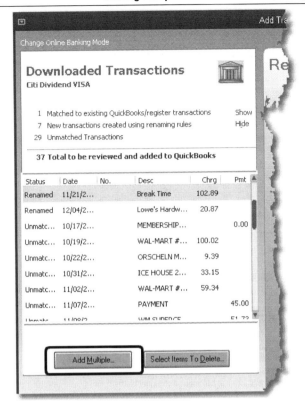

2. **Click the Add Multiple button.**

The Add Multiple Transactions to QuickBooks window will open. It lists Renamed (New) and Unmatched transactions in the upper pane, and Matched transactions in the lower pane:

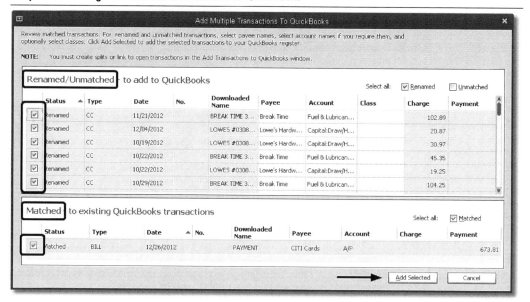

3. **Review and edit Renamed (New) and Unmatched transactions** as needed, then **check mark the ones you want to add to QuickBooks,** in the boxes along the window's left side.

   For Unmatched transactions especially, you need to select a Payee and an Account. Note that this window also has a column for assigning a Class if you want.

4. **Review Matched transactions,** and **check mark the ones you want to add to QuickBooks.**

5. **Click the Add Selected button** to add the checkmarked transactions to QuickBooks.

   QuickBooks will add the transactions and close the window.

Deleting Downloaded Transactions You Don't Need

Sometimes a download may include some old transactions which you have already reconciled in QuickBooks. This is especially likely the first time you download transactions for an account.

Though QuickBooks compares downloaded transactions against existing transactions in an attempt to avoid adding duplicates, it only compares against existing transactions *which have not yet been reconciled.* So it is possible that some of the downloaded transactions will match (be duplicates of) existing transactions, without

QuickBooks "seeing" them as matching. As a result, these downloaded transactions will show up in either Unmatched or New transactions in the Add Transactions to QuickBooks window 36. But they *should not be added,* because doing that would duplicate existing transactions.

The simple solution is to delete these would-be duplicates rather than adding them. Here's how to delete downloaded transactions you don't want to add to QuickBooks:

1. **Open the Add Transactions to QuickBooks window,** as described earlier 36.

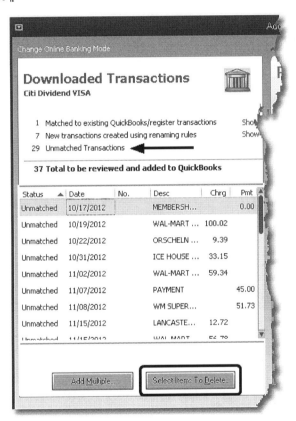

2. **Click on the *Unmatched transactions* link** in the upper left pane of the window, to display the list of unmatched transactions in the lower left pane.

    Optionally, you may also click on the **Show** link on the *New transactions created using renaming rules* line to include them. (Unmatched, New, and Matched transactions can be safely deleted without affecting any existing transactions in Quick-Books.)

3. **Click the Select Items to Delete button,** to open the Select Items to Delete window.

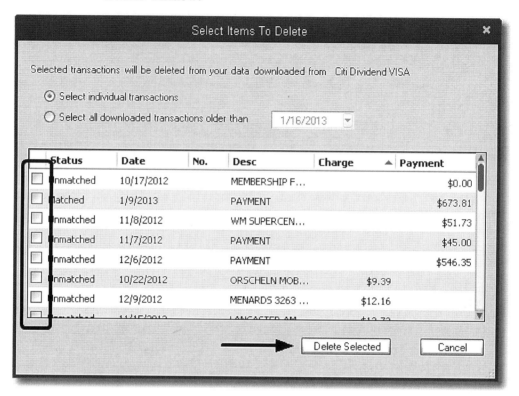

4. **Check mark the boxes** beside transactions you want to delete.

5. **Click the Delete Selected button** to delete the transactions you checkmarked.

Tips for Working with Downloaded Transactions

Working with downloaded transactions will be faster after you've done it a few times

Downloading will become easier and you'll be more efficient at it after you've done it a few times. Getting accustomed to its quirks and oddities takes a bit of practice. Also, your first few download sessions will take longer as you spend time creating renaming rules 55. Once you have established renaming rules for the vendors you most commonly do business with, the process will be faster and more streamlined.

The very first time you download, watch out for duplicates!

Depending on when you last reconciled the account, and the bank or credit card company's cut-off date for transactions to include in the download, your first download may contain transactions which QuickBooks is unable to match up with existing transactions.

> **How is that possible?** It is because *reconciled* transactions are excluded when QuickBooks compares downloaded transactions with existing transactions.

QuickBooks will put these seemingly unmatched transactions in either the Unmatched or New transactions category of the Add Transactions to QuickBooks window 36, so that you may add them to QuickBooks. But because they are duplicates of existing (reconciled) transactions, you need to delete them instead. For details on how to do that see *Deleting Downloaded Transactions You Don't Need* 50, earlier in this chapter.

> **If duplicate transactions get added, don't worry.** Spotting them in an account register is pretty easy: they won't have a reconciled checkmark (✔) yet their amount will be identical to a nearby transaction which <u>does</u> have a reconciled checkmark (✔). Once found, they are easy to delete. And if you don't find all of them immediately you'll catch the rest when you reconcile the account.

For what transaction types will I most likely save time, if I download them?

◆ In a typical small business situation, using QuickBooks correctly will mean that *many of your bank transactions may have already been entered manually* by the time you download transactions from the bank.

Normally you will have entered **deposits** in QuickBooks when you prepared physical deposits to take or send to the bank, and entered **checks** before printing them for mailing. Also, if you use online banking, you may have entered checks to be processed online as electronic transactions. Each of these activities creates a check or a deposit entry in QuickBooks. So when you add downloaded transactions, the matching process will ignore (and not add) many of them because a corresponding transaction entry will already exist in QuickBooks in many cases.

The point is that you cannot save much data entry effort by downloading transactions if you have already entered most of the same transactions manually.

◆ The story is a bit different for **handwritten checks** and **debit card purchases**. If you use many of either, you are much more likely to save time by downloading bank transactions. The reason is that neither of these are as likely to have been entered in Quick-Books prior to downloading transactions from the bank.

◆ Downloading **credit card** transactions will very likely yield time savings. They, too, are seldom entered in QuickBooks prior to downloading, so you may get the benefit of having the entire month's credit card transactions added to QuickBooks, with minimal effort on your part.

Applying Classes and Customer:Jobs to downloaded transactions

Downloaded transactions don't have Classes or Customer:Jobs assigned to them. If you want to apply these to your transactions, you need to do that either during the process of adding downloaded transactions⎡35⎤ to QuickBooks, or by editing transaction details after the transactions have been added⎡69⎤—which will be discussed in chapter 6.

CHAPTER 5

Renaming Rules: "Aliases" for Customer/Vendor Names

About this chapter	This chapter tells how to create and edit renaming rules, which are the *single most important feature* for automating the process of adding downloaded bank or credit card transactions to QuickBooks.

Renaming Rules: What and Why

 Renaming rules were called *aliases* in earlier QuickBooks versions.

 Renaming rules were enhanced in QuickBooks 2013. If you are using an older version some of the features described in this chapter may not be available to you.

What are renaming rules?

When completing Unmatched transactions39, if you select a Customer, Vendor, or other name in the Payee field of a downloaded transaction QuickBooks will automatically create a renaming rule. The renaming rule is simply an "alias" for that Customer or Vendor name. It tells QuickBooks which Customer or Vendor to associate with a downloaded transaction when a particular spelling of the name is found in the Payee field.

For instance, suppose a downloaded transaction has "Albert's Shell Oil Co." in the Payee field, and you have "Albert's Shell" in your Vendors list. The renaming rule tells QuickBooks that downloaded transactions with "Albert's Shell Oil Co." in the Payee field actually refer to the "Albert's Shell" vendor.

What can renaming rules do for you?

Renaming rules help to automate the process of adding downloaded bank or credit card transactions to QuickBooks. They:

◆ **Automate preparing downloaded transactions for adding to QuickBooks.**

When a renaming rule exists which matches the spelling of a name in the Payee field of a downloaded transaction, Quick-Books will associate the appropriate Customer, Vendor, or other name with the transaction. It will also assign an account to the transaction—the same account as was used in the most recent transaction involving that Customer or Vendor. The result is a new transaction with a Payee and Account assigned, ready for adding to QuickBooks.

QuickBooks automatically compares *all* of the downloaded transactions against your renaming rules, and prepares a new transaction wherever a renaming rule can be applied. These new transactions are placed in the *New transactions created using renaming rules* category (listed in the upper left pane of the Add Transactions to QuickBooks window).

 Transactions created by using renaming rules are created automatically—with no intervention by you—so it's a good idea to review them 46 before they are added to QuickBooks. Sometimes the account assigned by QuickBooks may not be what you want.

◆ **Let you automatically match several different payee name spellings with a single QuickBooks Customer or Vendor.**

An example will explain this best...

Suppose you frequently make purchases at several different NAPA auto parts stores. You have a "NAPA" vendor name in the Vendors list and apply it to any transaction involving a NAPA store. You've used a debit card to make purchases at a couple different NAPA stores in the past month, and those debit card transactions will be included in your monthly download of transactions from the bank.

An important thing to understand about downloaded trans-actions is that their data fields can contain whatever information the vendor and/or your bank or credit card company chose to put there! The Payee field, for example, will often contain information *in addition to the payee name*—maybe a store number ("NAPA Store 283"), or a city or location ID ("NAPA - Webb City"), or even the transaction date or a transaction number of some kind ("NAPA - 1143678486").

In the case of our example, it is very likely that the Payee field *will not* simply match the "NAPA" name in your Vendors list. More likely, the Payee name may be something like "NAPA Store 1147" in one of the transactions, "NAPA Store 283" in another, and so on.

This is exactly the kind of situation solved by renaming rules. By associating the "NAPA" vendor with transactions involving "NAPA Store 1147" *and* "NAPA Store 283" you will automatically be creating renaming rules which tell QuickBooks that whenever either of those payee names is encountered, they refer to the "NAPA" name in your Vendors list.

What if the Payee name is *slightly different* in every transaction from a certain vendor?

This can happen when the date ("NAPA - 12/14/2012") or a transaction number ("NAPA - 1143678486", etc.) is included in the Payee field of downloaded transactions—which makes the Payee name slightly different in each one.

The question is: Will having the Payee spelled a bit differently like this, keep your renaming rules from working?

The answer: Yes...or no...depending on which QuickBooks version you use:

◆ **In QuickBooks versions prior to 2013,** having slightly different information in the Payee field of transactions from a particular vendor made renaming rules worthless for that vendor, because QuickBooks could not make partial matches on the Payee field. In those cases all transactions for such vendors were unmatched and had to have the correct name assigned to the Payee field manually.

◆ **QuickBooks 2013 and later versions** have a solution for this problem. They support renaming rules which can match just a part of the Payee field if you want. In our example, the renaming rule could be edited to match any transaction with "NAPA" at the beginning of the Payee field. That would allow it to match all NAPA store transactions regardless of other information included in the field, such as store IDs or transaction numbers.

How to Manage and Edit Renaming Rules

You can view, edit, and delete renaming rules from the Add Trans-actions to QuickBooks window.

1. **Open the Add Transactions to QuickBooks window,** as described in the prior chapter⌐36⌐.

2. **Click on the Renaming Rules link** in the upper right corner of the window.

The Edit Renaming Rules window will open.

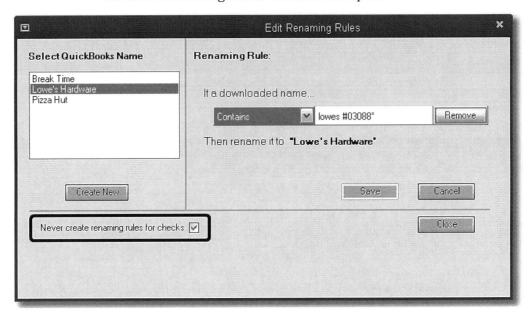

What is the purpose of the *Never create renaming rules for checks* setting?

Check marking this box, which is toward the bottom of the Edit Renaming Rules window, prevents QuickBooks from creating renaming rules for down-loaded transactions which have the word "Check" in the Payee field. This setting is **highly recommended for most users** but depends on what your bank puts in the Payee field of check transactions.

Suppose for instance, that your bank always puts the word "Check" along with the check number in Payee field, such as "Check #4435". Further, suppose that while adding Unmatched transactions you complete this check by assigning "Miller Lumber Co." as the payee.

As you may recall, when you assign a Payee to an Unmatched transaction QuickBooks will automatically add a new renaming rule to associate the original Payee name (in this case, "Check #4435") with the vendor name you assigned ("Miller Lumber Co.").

The problem with letting QuickBooks add a renaming rule for a payee named "Check #4435" is that this payee name *won't ever be encountered again*—or at least it is not very likely. If you write ten checks to Miller Lumber Company during the year, QuickBooks will add *ten different renaming rules* for the "Miller Lumber Co." vendor—each of them differing only by their check number!

An *even worse* problem is possible...

Suppose your bank simply puts "CHECK" in the Payee field of all check transactions. If you assign the "Miller Lumber Co." vendor to the first check you process, QuickBooks will create a renaming rule which assigns that vendor to *all downloaded checks!* Why? Because all of them have the same payee name, "CHECK".

The solution to both problems, is to use the ***Never create renaming rules for checks*** setting, which prevents QuickBooks from adding renaming rules when the Payee field contains the word "Check".

Editing a Renaming Rule

Editing a Renaming Rule can make it apply to a wider range of customer or vendor name variations, to better automate the process of downloading transactions.

1. **Open the Add Transactions to QuickBooks window** 36, as described in the prior chapter.

2. **Click on the Renaming Rules link** in the upper right corner of the window.

The Edit Renaming Rules window will open.

3. In the left pane of the Edit Renaming Rules window, **click on a QuickBooks Name** (Customer, Vendor, etc.) to work with.

The right pane of the window will then show the renaming rules defined for the name you selected.

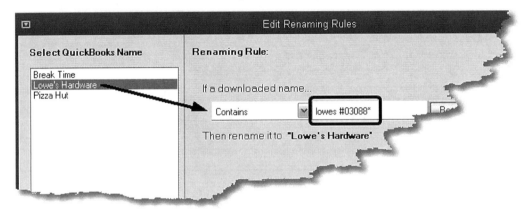

The rule in this example applies the "Lowes Hardware" vendor name to transactions with "lowes #03088*" in their Payee field. But we can edit the rule to make it work for transactions from *any* Lowe's store.

4. **Edit the text of the rule** so that instead of "lowes #03088*" it reads simply "lowes".

5. **Click the down-arrow to the left of the text**, to see the list of matching options.

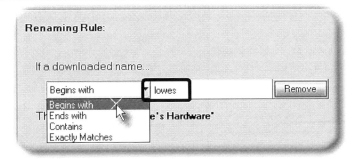

6. Select **Begins with** from the list of matching options.

This will cause QuickBooks to compare the rule's text with only the beginning part of the Payee field in downloaded transactions. In this case, any transaction which begins with "lowes" (upper *or* lower case) will be matched with the "Lowe's Hardware" vendor.

The other matching options are self explanatory and work similarly to *Begins with*.

Creating a New Renaming Rule

In addition to the renaming rules created automatically by Quick-Books, you can create additional rules of your own.

1. **Open the Add Transactions to QuickBooks window** 36, as described in the prior chapter.

2. **Click on the Renaming Rules link** in the upper right corner of the window.

The Edit Renaming Rules window will open.

3. In the Edit Renaming Rules window, **click the Create New button.**

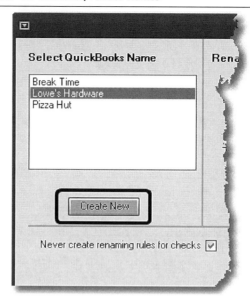

QuickBooks will display blank fields in the right pane, for
defining a new rule.

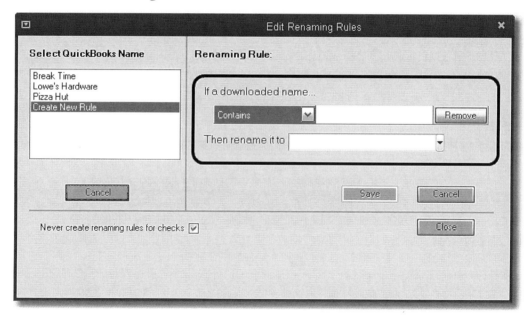

4. **Choose a matching type (Begins with, Contains, etc.), enter the text to
   be matched, and select a QuickBooks name (Customer or Vendor) to
   apply** when the rule matches the Payee field's text.

Here's a *Contains* rule which will match "lumber" anywhere in the Payee field of a downloaded transaction and replace it with the vendor name "Miller Lumber Co.":

5. **Click the Save button** to save the new rule.

Note that when multiple rules are defined for a name, they are all listed together in the right pane. Here's how the window might look with two rules defined for the "Miller Lumber Co." vendor:

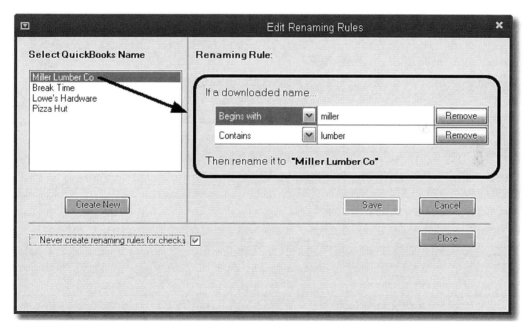

Deleting a Renaming Rule

1. **Open the Add Transactions to QuickBooks window** 36, as described in the prior chapter.

2. **Click on the Renaming Rules link** in the upper right corner of the window.

The Edit Renaming Rules window will open.

3. In the Edit Renaming Rules window, **click on the QuickBooks name you want to work with.**

The right pane of the window will then list the renaming rule(s) defined for that name.

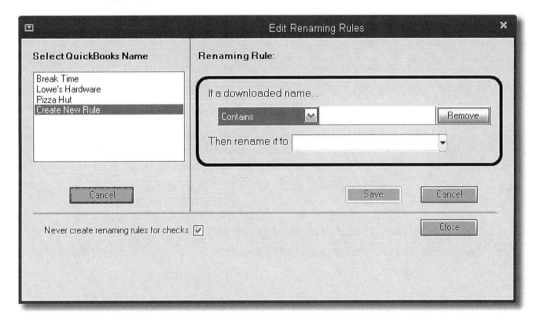

4. Click the *Remove* button beside the rule you want to delete.

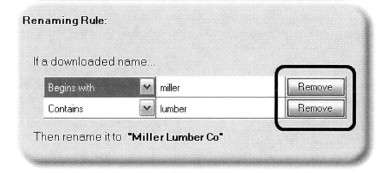

5. **Click the Save button** (near the bottom of the window) to make the deletion permanent.

This page is intentionally blank.

CHAPTER 6

Special Topics for Online & Downloaded Transactions

About this chapter	This chapter explores miscellaneous topics about working with online (electronic) transactions, and transactions you have downloaded and added to QuickBooks.

Reconcile and Prepare Reports...Often!

With so many automated features for adding downloaded trans-actions to QuickBooks, something is bound to go wrong at times:

◆ A duplicate check or deposit entry may be added when Quick-Books doesn't correctly match a downloaded transaction with an existing check or deposit entry.

◆ Renaming rules can automatically apply the wrong name. For instance, suppose you set up a renaming rule which matches the "Lowe's Hardware" vendor with any downloaded transaction having "lowes" at the beginning of the Payee field. Unfortunately (and unintentionally) that same rule will also match downloaded transactions having "Lowesmann Landscaping Supply" in the Payee field!

◆ QuickBooks may sometimes apply the wrong account—an account you didn't intend—to transactions it has created based on your renaming rules.

◆ There can be errors in the transaction data you download from the bank or credit card company. Though rare, their computers and operators are subject to making errors too.

Don't forget to reconcile!

If you talk to accountants who use the transaction downloading features a lot, you'll likely hear about the importance of reconciling accounts to catch errors. Reconciling is a sure-fire way to catch things like duplicated transactions.

Reports can help too

How do you notice that the wrong account or vendor has been assigned? The easiest way to catch those errors is usually by preparing QuickBooks reports—and doing it often. Once a month is good, because catching errors is easier when you only have a month's worth of transactions to look at. Waiting until year's end is too late: the volume of transactions to review and the amount of time that has passed will hinder your ability to notice errors.

What kinds of reports? Generally, you need to prepare QuickBooks Detail reports—the kind that list transactions individually. The Profit & Loss Detail report, for example, is good for noticing transactions posted to the wrong accounts. A QuickReport is also good for this—you can generate one from the account's Register window. It will list transactions individually for whatever date range you choose, and includes detail columns like Account, Name (Customer, Vendor, etc.), Class, and so on.

Finding Downloaded & Online Transactions in an Account Register

A Register lists all of an account's transactions. Register windows are available for balance sheet accounts (asset, liability, and equity accounts), but not for income or expense accounts. To open an account's Register, click on the account in the Chart of Accounts window (Lists > Chart of Accounts), then type *Ctrl-R*. Or, simply double-click the account.

One of the Register window's features is a checkmark column, which indicates the reconciled status of each transaction: a checkmark (✔) means the transaction has been reconciled, while an asterisk (*) means it has not yet been reconciled.

With the addition of online banking features in newer versions of QuickBooks, the checkmark column has an additional purpose. When it contains a lightning bolt symbol (⚡), it indicates a transaction which is not yet reconciled *and* is either (1) a downloaded transaction or (2) an electronic transaction, such as an online bill payment.

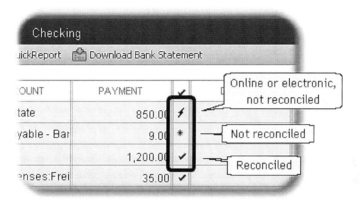

⭐ **The lightning bolt symbol (⚡) is shown *only until the transaction has been reconciled*** (i.e., until it is marked as having cleared the bank or credit card account). Once reconciled, the lightning bolt (⚡) is replaced by a checkmark (✔) and you can no longer distinguish the transaction from a manually entered one by looking at the account Register.

Adding Detail to Downloaded Transactions... Another (Better?) Way

Compared to the QuickBooks forms you normally use for editing transactions, the Add Transactions to QuickBooks window [36] can feel limited and confining: the Payee, Account, Memo, and other fields are all a bit small. Many people feel they simply cannot see enough information at once—they say it feels like trying to read a newspaper through a keyhole!

If you'd like a more comfortable (spacious and familiar) place for filling in the details of downloaded transactions, you can have it. The trick is to just add the minimum amount of detail required to get downloaded transactions added to QuickBooks, then edit the transactions on forms you are accustomed to—Write Checks, Enter Credit Card Charges, etc.—to add more detail. Here's how:

1. In the Add Transactions to QuickBooks window⌐36¬, **click on the Add Multiple button.**

   The Add Multiple Transactions to QuickBooks window⌐48¬ will open, listing all of the downloaded transactions.

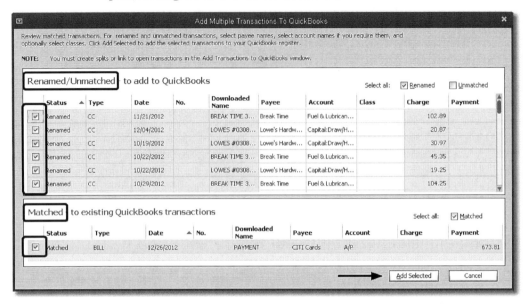

2. **Review and edit Renamed (New) and Unmatched transactions,** *supplying the minimum detail required* for adding the transactions to QuickBooks.

   At a minimum, QuickBooks requires selecting an Account for each transaction. Depending on your QuickBooks Preference settings (Edit > Preferences), you may also have to select a Payee (Customer, Vendor, etc.), and possibly a Class.

3. **Check mark all transactions,** in both the upper and lower panes of the window.

4. **Click the Add Selected button.**

   QuickBooks will add all of the checkmarked transactions and will close the window.

5. **Click the Done button** in the Add Transactions to QuickBooks window, to close it.

6. **Open a Register window for the account you are working with.**

   For example, if the downloaded transactions were added to a credit card account, you could open its Register window by (1) opening the Chart of Accounts (Lists > Chart of Accounts), then (2) double-clicking the credit card account, or selecting it and then typing *Ctrl-R*.

7. **Scroll upward in the Register window,** until the first recently-downloaded transaction is in view.

The downloaded transactions added in step 4 should be easy to find, because each of them should have a lightning bolt symbol (⚡) in its checkmark column:

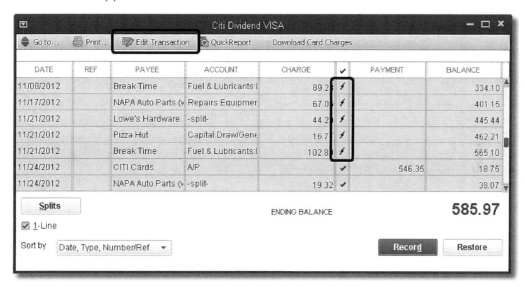

⭐ **Later, after you've reconciled the account,** the lightning bolt symbols (⚡) will be changed to a checkmark (✔) for all transactions included in the reconcile, making it more difficult to distinguish downloaded transactions from those you have added manually.

8. **Click on the first recently-added (downloaded) transaction**, to select it.

9. **Click the Edit Transaction button** at the top of the Register window.

An edit window will open for the transaction, as shown below. Since only an Account was selected when this transaction was added, only an account and an amount appear in the detail area:

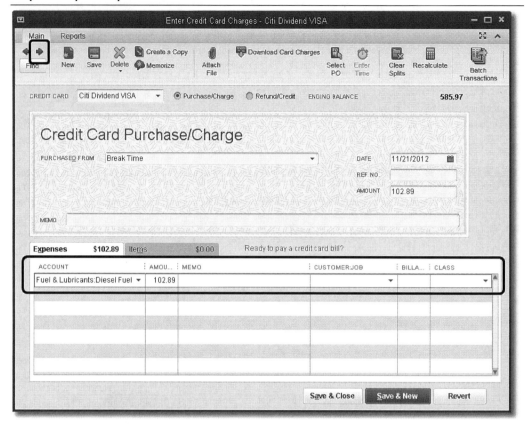

10. **Make changes in the transaction, adding any information you want it to have.**

    Here's the detail line of the same transaction after adding a Memo, Customer:Job, and Class name:

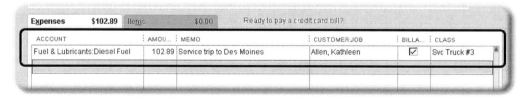

11. **Click the Next arrow** at the top of the window, to save your changes and move to the next transaction.

If you haven't entered any transactions manually (as might be the case for a credit card account) the downloaded transactions should be in sequential order in the Register, so clicking the Next arrow should move to the next downloaded transaction. If you *have* entered some transactions manually, you may need to click Next a few times to find the next downloaded transaction to edit.

12. When you run out of transactions to edit, **go back to the Register window, look for other transactions to edit, and edit them as appropriate.**

If you are working with a bank account, for instance, you may have been editing checks in step 8, on the Write Checks form. Because deposits are edited on the Make Deposits form, they will have been bypassed and will still need to be reviewed and/or edited.

Connecting Downloaded Payment Transactions to Bills

Suppose you've entered a monthly utility bill—let's say, your electric bill—as a Bill in QuickBooks (**Vendors > Enter Bills**):

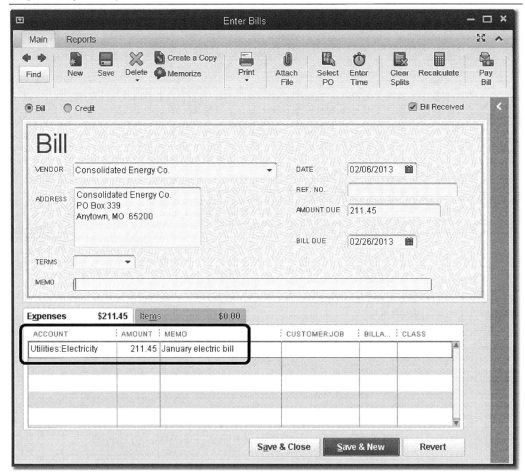

A week or so later you are driving by the electric company office and decide to stop and pay the bill, to assure that your payment isn't late. Not having your checkbook along, you pay by credit card. Later in the month, you download credit card transactions and add them to QuickBooks.

At this point you have a problem. When you open the Pay Bills window (**Vendors > Pay Bills**) you see that the electric bill you entered is still listed as an unpaid bill. Why? Because QuickBooks doesn't mark a bill as "Paid" until it is connected with a payment—in this case, with one of the credit card transactions you downloaded.

Normally a payment gets connected to a bill *automatically* in Quick-Books, but that only happens if you enter the payment in the Pay Bills window. If you download transactions without first entering a payment in Pay Bills, you will have to *manually* connect the payment transaction to the bill.

Let's look at the recommended (automatic) way to have a payment connected with a bill, then later, see how to connect them manually.

 Though the examples below deal with credit card bill payments, the same techniques would apply to bill payments made by **check or debit card.**

Connecting Bills and Payments Automatically

Using the Pay Bills window (Vendors > Pay Bills) to enter a payment automatically connects the payment with a bill. If you pay a bill by credit card, debit card, or handwritten check, it's best to enter the payment in the Pay Bills window soon after making payment— really, any time *before* downloading bank or credit card transactions. That way, the process of adding downloaded transactions to QuickBooks will simply match your manually-entered bill payment with the appropriate downloaded transaction, and no transactions will be duplicated.

Here's how to enter the manual payment, for a bill paid by credit card:

1. **Open the Pay Bills window** (Vendors > Pay Bills).

2. **Select a bill** to be paid.

3. In the Payment area, **select Credit Card as the Method** and **choose the credit card account to use for making payment, in the Account field.**

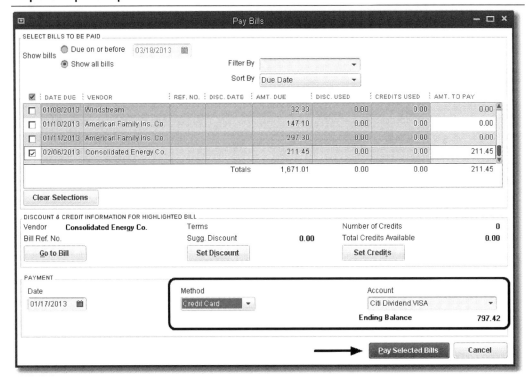

4. Click the Pay Selected Bills button.

QuickBooks will create a transaction which pays the bill (reduces Accounts Payable by the amount of the bill) and charges the credit card account for the same amount. This transaction "connects" the bill and the credit card payment, allowing QuickBooks to mark the bill as "Paid" and remove it from the Pay Bills window.

What will happen later when you download credit card transactions? Since you've already entered the bill payment, the corresponding downloaded transaction will simply be matched up with it —not added as a new transaction entry—and your entries will all be as they should be.

Connecting Bills and Payments Manually

If:

◆ You have paid some bills by credit card, debit card, or hand-written check, and

◆ You *have not* entered those payments in the Pay Bills window, and

◆ You have downloaded and added transactions to QuickBooks, for the credit card or bank account,

Then:

◆ You will have to manually connect the downloaded payment transactions with their corresponding bills.

★ **If you've downloaded transactions but *have not yet added them*** to QuickBooks, you can still use the recommended approach described earlier 75. That is, *before adding* the downloaded transactions to QuickBooks, use the Pay Bills window to manually enter the payments that were made by credit card, debit card, or handwritten check. Then when you add the downloaded transactions, they will be matched up with your manual bill payment entries.

Preparing a credit card transaction for connecting to a bill

★ **Though this example deals with a credit card bill payment,** the same techniques would be used if the payment had been made by **check or debit card.**

1. **Open a Register window** for the credit card account.

   In the Chart of Accounts window (**Lists > Chart of Accounts**), select the credit card account by clicking on it, then type *Ctrl-R*.

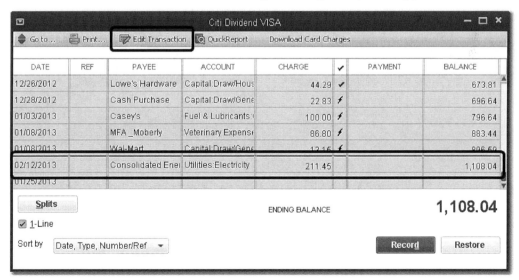

2. **Click on the transaction you want to edit,** to prepare it for matching with a bill.

3. **Click the Edit Transaction button** at the top of the Register window.

The Enter Credit Card Charges window will open, so that you can edit the transaction.

Before editing, the credit card entry shown below posts expense directly to the Utilities:Electricity account. Since our original Bill entry has already posted expense to that account, we need to select a different account in the Account field—which is also the key to connecting this credit card transaction entry to the bill.

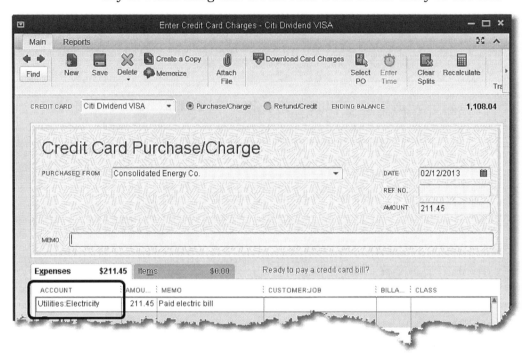

4. *On the Items tab,* **delete all Item lines, if any.**

5. *On the Expenses tab,* **delete all of the lines except one.** On that line, **select Accounts Payable** in the Account column and **select the appropriate vendor name** in the Customer:Job field.

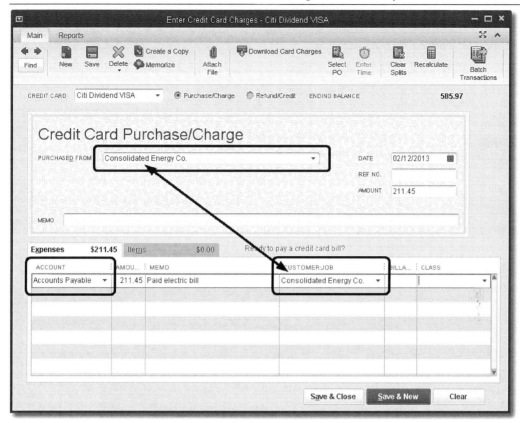

Note again, that Accounts Payable is now selected as the account *instead of* Utilities:Electricity, the account to which this credit card entry was originally posted.

6. **Double-check to be sure** that the name of the vendor to whom the bill is owed is selected in the Purchased From field *and* in the Customer:Job column.

7. **Click the Save & Close button or the Save & New button** to save your changes.

Repeat these steps for each transaction you need to connect to a bill.

Connecting a credit card payment to a bill

⭐ **Though this example deals with a bill paid by credit card,** the same techniques would be used if the bill had been paid by **check or debit card.**

The steps above converted the credit card payments into credits on account for the vendors involved. Now, each of those vendor accounts has an unused credit on account and also an unpaid bill for the same amount (i.e., the original Bill entry).

All that's left to do is to connect the appropriate credits and bills so that QuickBooks can mark the bills as paid:

1. **Open the Pay Bills window** (Vendors > Pay Bills).

2. **Checkmark a bill** to select it for payment.

   A credit amount should appear on the Total Credits Available line, toward the lower right side of the window. It should be for the same amount as the bill if you properly edited the corresponding credit card transaction as described in the section above 77.

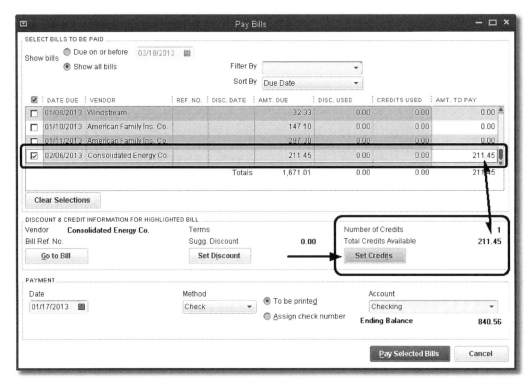

3. **Click the Set Credits button.**

   The Discounts and Credits window will open, displaying the available credit amounts for this account.

4. In the Discounts and Credits window, **checkmark the line which shows the credit from the credit card transaction.**

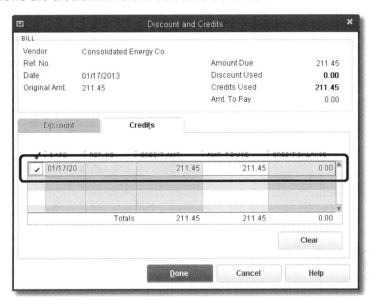

5. **Click the Done button** to close the Discounts and Credits window.

In the Pay Bills window, the Amt. to Pay column now shows 0.00 for the selected bill.

6. In the Pay Bills window, **click the Pay Selected Bills button.**

QuickBooks will complete payment of the bill by applying the credit you selected in step 4 and marking the bill as Paid, and will close the Pay Bills window.

Another option: Delete the bill

Besides the two approaches described above, another alternative is to simply delete the original Bill entry.

If an expense account was assigned to the credit card transaction you downloaded—like the Utilities:Electricity account in this example—the expense would be properly recorded, so deleting the Bill would solve the problem of having an unpaid bill in the Pay Bills window. However, there are a couple potential problems to consider:

1. **Deleting the bill now, could lead to confusion later.** The deleted bill would simply be missing from reports showing your Accounts Payable history for the electric company (Consolidated Energy Co. in this

example), possibly sending you—or someone else—on a "wild goose chase" to find out why no bill had been entered for that month.

2. **Deleting the bill could cause expense to be recorded in the wrong accounting period,** if you keep records on an accrual basis.

   Suppose your business uses a calendar fiscal year (January 1 through December 31). Also suppose that the original bill was dated December 23 and the credit card payment transaction was dated January 4. The credit card transaction would record expense in the current year, while the original bill recorded expense in the prior year. Simply deleting the bill rather than connecting it to the credit card payment would move the expense out of the prior accounting year and into the current one—which would be counter to accrual principles. (This is not a consideration if you are a cash-basis record keeper.)

CHAPTER 7

Electronic Transactions in Online Banking

<table>
<tr><td>**About this chapter**</td><td>This chapter shows how to enter transactions in QuickBooks for processing online (as electronic transactions).</td></tr>
</table>

Entering Electronic Transactions in QuickBooks

Problem   **How do I enter transactions in QuickBooks so that they will be processed electronically by my bank or credit card company?**

Solution   Enter them on the same forms you use for other transactions—most often, on the Write Checks or Transfer Funds form—but mark them for online processing so that they will be processed as electronic transactions.

Discussion   Electronic transactions do away with the need to send payments through the mail. In QuickBooks they are entered just like other transactions, except that you must remember to mark them for online processing.

Unless you've subscribed to an online bill payment service [87], your electronic transactions will generally be limited to (1) paying the bank or credit card company, and (2) transferring funds between accounts *at the same financial institution,* such as from a savings or money market account to the business checking account at your bank. Also, note that both of the accounts involved in the transfer must be set up for online access [23] in QuickBooks.

How to Enter an Electronic Funds Transfer

Here's how to enter a QuickBooks transaction that will transfer funds between two accounts at the same bank, when processed online as an electronic transaction.

⭐ This example deals with what is often called **online banking**. To electronically transfer funds between accounts at *different* banks you normally must be subscribed to an **online bill payment** service.

1. **Choose** Banking > Transfer Funds.

   The Transfer Funds Between Accounts window will open.

2. **Fill in the fields,** identifying the accounts involved in the transfer, and check marking the *Online Funds Transfer* box.

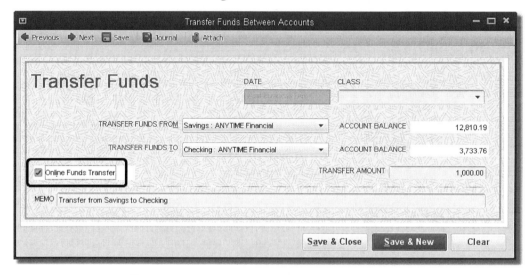

🔺 **Forgetting to checkmark the *Online Funds Transfer* box** will only transfer funds *between your QuickBooks accounts,* not between the real-world accounts at your bank!

🔧 **If no online connection has been set up for one of the accounts you have selected,** QuickBooks will notify you and will remove the *Online Funds Transfer* check mark, preventing the transaction from being processed electronically.

3. **Click Save & Close** to save the transaction and close the window,
    or
    Save & New to save it and clear the form, to allow entering
    another transfer.

4. **What happens next? Nothing!**

    Simply *entering* an electronic funds transfer does not accomplish
    the transfer. The transaction won't be processed until you send/
    receive transactions in the Online Banking Center (Banking >
    Online Banking > Online Banking Center).

    **After sending an electronic transaction you cannot make changes
    in it** except for editing the Memo field. Before sending it though,
    anything about the transaction can be edited; or, you may delete it
    entirely.

Other Examples of Electronic Transactions

As mentioned earlier, unless you've signed up for an online bill
paying service your electronic transactions will mostly be limited to
transferring funds between accounts within your bank, or paying
your credit card balance. For information about other kinds of
electronic transactions see chapter 8, Online Bill Payment and
QuickBooks 87.

This page is intentionally blank.

Online Bill Payment and QuickBooks

About Online Bill Payment and QuickBooks

Paying bills online often (but not always) comes with some costs. In fact, the monthly and per-transaction fees charged by some online bill payment services can seem expensive when you first encounter them. But for any expense, what you pay has to be balanced against the benefits you receive, to decide whether the expense is justified. Many people find that the time, effort, postage, and paper they save by paying bills online more than makes up for what it costs.

Questions & Answers

Is online bill payment right for me? ...How do I decide?

This management decision is like most of the others you face: getting information about the *costs* of using an online bill payment service is easy. Any online bill payment service provider can tell you approximately what their monthly charges would be for your business. What's not so easy is *placing a value on the benefits* of using online bill payment.

Potential benefits include:

◆ **Time savings** due to less paper handling and a reduced need to print and mail checks.

◆ **Time savings and reduced errors** due to less data entry—especially if the online bill payment service is tightly integrated with QuickBooks, so that transactions, customer and vendor names and addresses, and so on, only have to be entered once.

◆ **Reduced expenses** for postage, envelopes and mailing, check forms, and printing (ink or toner cartridges, etc.)

◆ **Better management of cash flow and operating credit,** by being able to make payments exactly when you choose.

> ★ **Most online payment services let you "calendarize" bill payments.** You can set up a payment to be made on a specific date, and the funds will be transferred on that exact date. You no longer need to worry about when to mail a check to be sure it reaches the payee before the payment's due date!

Because most of these benefits are difficult to quantify, your best guide to their value is likely to be your "feel" for them. And the only way to get that "feel" is to try an online payment service. As management experiments go, a three-month test of online bill payment isn't very expensive. Many services even offer a free month or two when you sign up, which will make your test cost even less.

If I sign up for an online bill payment service, should I pay all of my bills through it?

While it may be *possible* to pay all of your bills through an online service, generally that's not something you will do, for several reasons:

◆ Monthly fees for online payment services usually allow **up to a certain number of transactions per month** (25, for instance). If you make more payments than that during the month, you may pay additional per-transaction fees of $0.50 or so. To keep fees to a minimum, you need to avoid exceeding the number of transactions allowed per month.

◆ Bills are paid electronically, usually via ACH transactions [8] (electronic payments sent directly to the payee's bank account), so **making an online payment requires information about the payee's bank account or other payment destination.** Having that information available for everyone you need to pay is not always practical. In some cases it is simpler to just print a check from QuickBooks, and mail it.

◆ Though increasingly rare, **not everyone can except ACH transactions.** As long as you can provide a name and address for the payee, the online bill payment service should be able to mail them a physical check. But that will typically cost you an additional transaction fee of $1 or more. So you may simply want to print a check from QuickBooks and mail it yourself.

Do I have to use the QuickBooks Bill Pay Service?
Or can I use another service and just have it synchronize with QuickBooks?

Intuit markets the QuickBooks Bill Pay Service through Web page links that you will encounter at various places within QuickBooks. Being able to just click a link makes signing up for Intuit's online bill payment service easy.

But you have a lot of other choices for vendors of online bill payment services. One may be your bank: many banks now offer online bill payment, often as a free or added-fee service in addition to their other online banking services. Also, you can find online bill payment services on the Web. As this is written, probably the best-known of these is www.Bill.com.

> ⭐ **Some people switch banks** to get one that offers free or low-cost online bill payment. Fees and availability vary, so it pays to shop around.

Most online bill payment services can synchronize with QuickBooks —meaning you can download your online transactions and add them to QuickBooks. Some offer even better, more automated synchronization with QuickBooks. Before you sign up for any service, be sure to ask about the level of QuickBooks synchronization they offer.

How do I sign up with an online bill payment service?

You sign up with the service provider, which may be your bank or someone else.

◆ **Signing up with your bank** should be simple, because they already have your name, address, account numbers, and other required information. You will have to register for an online account if you don't already have one, sign up for their online bill payment service, and if the service is not free you will have to agree to have the monthly fees automatically withdrawn from your account. In most cases you will do all of this from the bank's Web site.

After signing up you will be able to pay bills directly, set up bills for scheduled payment on dates you chooose, and transfer funds between accounts—even accounts at other banks, usually—and do all of that from the bank's Web site.

As for synchronizing with QuickBooks, since all of your bill payment activities will draw funds from an account(s) at your bank, you can capture the online payment transactions as part of your regular transaction downloads from the bank for that account(s).

◆ **Signing up with another service provider** is almost as easy, except that you will have to provide them with more information— things your bank already has, like your name and address, bank routing and account numbers, and so on. The rest of the sign-up process will be similar and you will have to agree to similar terms, such as automatic withdrawal of the monthly service fees from your bank account.

Once you've completed signup, paying bills and transferring funds online will work about the same as described above for banks. However, the level of QuickBooks integration provided by different services can vary a lot.

 www.Bill.com, for instance, goes well beyond simple trans- action downloading to synchronize with QuickBooks. With one click it updates your QuickBooks file for changes in Customers, Vendors, Bills, Invoices, etc., while you were using www.Bill. com.

Likewise, Intuit's QuickBooks Bill Pay Service (www. quickbooks.intuit.com/product/add_ons/bill_pay.jsp) directly updates account registers, etc., for your bill payment activities. And since it works entirely from within QuickBooks, there's no need for additional synchronization with your Customers, Vendors, and other lists.

How do I "connect" with a person or business to pay them online?

Paying someone electronically requires more information than you would need for paying them by check. The electronic payment pro- cess must have an "electronic address" for the person or business you are paying—their bank routing number and account number, or other electronically identifiable account or address information.

The steps required for getting that "electronic address" information depends partly on the assistance available from your online bill payment provider. Here are some examples:

◆ Some providers' Web sites have features that help with finding payee account information. They may let you search for payees based on a company or individual name, ZIP code, or other information. Once found, you can save the payee information in your personal list of payees, so that the next time you need to send them a payment you can simply choose them from the list.

> ⭐ **Another piece of information you'll need for most payees** is the account number they use for identifying *your* account with them. That's necessary so that the electronic payments you send can be properly credited to your account.

◆ If a payee can't be found by searching, you may be allowed to directly enter their name, address, and bank routing and account numbers, then save them in your personal list of payees. However, in most cases the online payment provider's system can gather this information for you, through the search process described above. You'll rarely (if ever) have to manually enter payee account numbers.

> ⭐ **You can find the routing number for any U.S. bank** at 🌐 www.routingnumbers.org, as well as a number of other sites on the Web.

◆ When using the QuickBooks Bill Pay Service, you set up payee information—name, address, etc.—in the Vendors list within QuickBooks. Since you probably already have this information entered for most vendors, it won't involve much extra work. As mentioned above though, there's one extra piece of information you need to add to the Vendor record: the account number the payee uses for identifying *your* account with them. (You'll find it on the Payment Settings tab in QuickBooks 2013, or the Additional Info tab in prior versions.)

Web-Based Online Payment Services

Bill payment services which operate from a Web site all work a bit differently, depending on how the service provider has designed their site. In general, you log in to their Web site, then use the site's features for entering and scheduling payments, getting reports, and so on.

Common features

Online bill payment services usually offer most or all of the following features:

◆ **Secure login** to the service's Web site. As with any Web-based service involving financial data, online payment services keep strict security measures in place to protect your account from unauthorized access.

◆ **Assistance with identifying payees,** often including capabilities to search for payees by name, ZIP code, and other information.

◆ **Ability to maintain your own personal list of payees,** to streamline the payment process. Once a payee has been added to your list, entering a payment for them will only require a couple mouse clicks.

◆ **Direct payment entry,** for making payments or transferring funds immediately.

◆ **Scheduled or "calendarized" payment entry,** for scheduling payments to be made later, on the date you specify.

◆ **Support for eBills,** including notifying you by email when an e-bill has been received, easy preparation of eBill payments, viewing and printing of eBills, etc.

> ★ **eBills are the electronic equivalent of paper bills.** Instead of coming to your mailbox eBills are sent to your bank or online bill payment service provider. You can view and pay eBills online, and can print them out if you wish. Most vendors who provide eBills let you sign up to receive them *in place of* paper bills, or to receive both if you prefer. For more information about eBills go to 🖄 www. ebillplace.com.

◆ **Reports** on scheduled payments, prior payments you have made, account balances, eBills you have received, and so on.

◆ **Synchronization with QuickBooks** may be accomplished by downloading (sending/receiving) transactions 30, or may be more sophisticated: some services provide one-click synchronization of QuickBooks lists (Customers, Vendors, etc.) and transaction data.

QuickBooks-Based Online Payment Services

With a Web-based online payment service, you enter payments on forms provided on the service provider's Web site. With a Quick-Books-based service, you enter electronic payments directly on familiar QuickBooks forms—Pay Bills, Write Checks, Transfer Funds, etc.—and check mark a box on the form to indicate that the payment is to be processed electronically.

A topic in the prior chapter showed how to enter an electronic funds transfer between two accounts at your bank, using the Transfer Funds form (Banking > Transfer Funds). The same approach works for entering payments to be processed by an online bill payment service, except that you can make payments to other businesses and individuals *outside of* your bank or credit card company.

How to Enter an Online Bill Payment in QuickBooks

This example is for a QuickBooks-based bill payment service—the QuickBooks Bill Pay Service offered by Intuit. The details of using a Web-based bill payment service will depend on the service you choose, so no specific example for using a Web-based service is provided here. The best places to find tutorials and examples for them is on the various bill payment services' Web sites.

Assuming you have entered a bill in QuickBooks (Vendors > Enter Bills), paying it online involves entering the payment on the Pay Bills form (Vendors > Pay Bills) and marking it for online (electronic) processing. Here are the steps involved:

1. **Choose** Vendors > Pay Bills.

   The Pay Bills window will open.

2. **Checkmark the bill** you want to pay, to select it for payment.

   In the Payment area of the window, **select *Online Bank Pmt*** as the Method, and in the Account field **select the account to use for making payment**—the Checking account is selected in the example below.

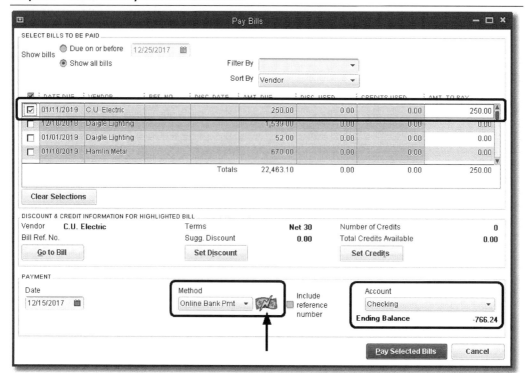

 Selecting *Online Bank Pmt* as the payment method causes QuickBooks to display a lightening-bolt graphic beside the Method box, as a reminder that the transaction will be processed electronically.

3. **Click the Pay Selected Bills button.**

   QuickBooks will create an electronic check entry, drawn on the Checking account in this example, for processing the next time you send/receive online transactions [30].

    The new check entry is no different from other checks in QuickBooks. You can see it in the Checking account's Register window and view it on the Write Checks form, as discussed in the Where is the electronic check [95] topic.

4. **Click the Cancel button** to close the Pay Bills window.

5. **What happens next? Nothing!**

   Simply *entering* an electronic payment does not cause the payment to be made. The transaction won't be processed until you

send/receive transactions 30 in the Online Banking Center
(**Banking > Online Banking > Online Banking Center**).

Where is the electronic check?

If you want to see the check QuickBooks prepared for the bill
payment, finding it is easy:

1. **Choose** Lists > Chart of Accounts to open the Chart of Accounts
    window.

    The Chart of Accounts window is one of several places from
    which you can open an account's Register.

2. **Click on the Checking account,** to select (highlight) it.

3. **Type** *Ctrl-R* to open the Checking account's Register window.

    The electronic check should be listed toward the bottom of the
    window if it was entered recently. Notice that the word "SEND"
    appears in the Number column, identifying it as a pending
    electronic transaction to be processed the next time you send/
    receive transactions 30 for the Checking account.

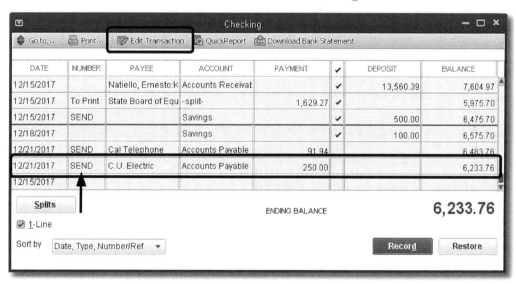

4. **Click on the check to select it, then click the Edit Transaction button** at
    the top of the Register window.

    The Write Checks window will open, showing the check's details.
    Notice that the Online Bank Pmt box (near the top of the win-

dow) is check marked and that a bank graphic appears on the check, as a reminder that check is to be processed electronically.

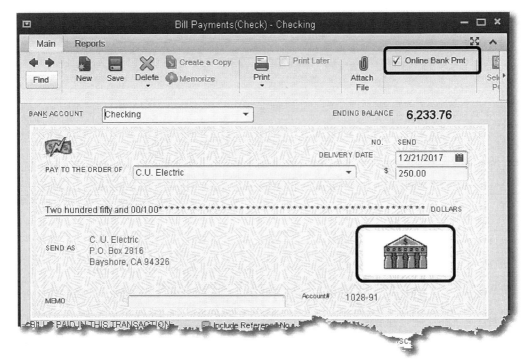

How to Enter an Online (Electronic) Check in QuickBooks

🔧 **This example is for a QuickBooks-based bill payment service**—the QuickBooks Bill Pay Service offered by Intuit. The details of using a Web-based bill payment service will depend on the service you choose, so no specific example for using a Web-based service is provided here. The best places to find tutorials and examples for them is on the various bill payment services' Web sites.

Sometimes you simply need to send an electronic payment to someone, which you can do by entering a check and marking it for processing online:

1. **Choose** Banking > Write Checks to open the Write Checks form.

2. **Fill in the form's fields,** as you would for any check, **being sure to check mark the *Pay Online* box** near the top of the form.

▲ **If you forget to check mark** *Pay Online* the check *will not be sent for electronic processing.* In other words, the payment won't happen!

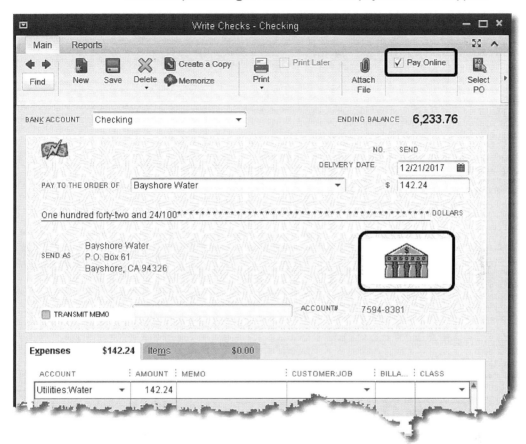

3. **Click Save & Close** to save the check entry and close the window, or
   Save & New to save it and clear the form to allow entering another check.

4. **What happens next? Nothing!**

   As with all electronic transactions entered in QuickBooks, simply *entering* an electronic check does not cause the payment to be made. The check won't be processed until you send/receive transactions⌐30⌐ in the Online Banking Center (**Banking > Online Banking > Online Banking Center**).

This page is intentionally blank.

CHAPTER 9

Appendix

Other Flagship Technologies Products

Here are other QuickBooks add-on software and book titles available from Flagship Technologies, Inc. Visit us on the Web at 📧 www. goflagship.com.

ManagePLUS for QuickBooks and **ManagePLUS Gold for QuickBooks** are add-on programs for gleaning management information from any set of QuickBooks accounting records, especially where the Classes feature of QuickBooks is used.

ManagePLUS gives you reports with per-unit revenue and cost information...things like fuel and maintenance costs per mile driven by trucks in a fleet, materials costs per unit of production in a factory, herbicide and fertilizer cost per acre or per bushel of corn production, and so on. The expanded quantity handling and reporting it offers—including support for storing two quantities in your QuickBooks transactions (usually, a weight and a count or quantity)—is something not found in any other QuickBooks add-on on the market.

ManagePLUS Gold adds cost accounting and activity-based costing features to the base ManagePLUS product. It gives you an easy drag-and-drop approach for allocating income and expense to Classes identified as cost centers and profit centers, provides spreadsheet-based profit analysis reports, and can send allocation transactions directly to QuickBooks, for additional reporting there.

ManagePLUS/Gold work with these Microsoft Windows editions of QuickBooks:

U.S.: Pro and Premier editions of QuickBooks 2003 and later, and Enterprise Solutions 3.0 and higher.

UK: Pro and Premier editions of UK QuickBooks 2004 and later.

Canadian: Pro and Premier editions of Canadian QuickBooks 2004 and later.

A **30-day free trial** is available to download—no commitment and no credit card required!

ManagePLUS/Gold on the Web:
    www.goflagship.com/products/mphome.htm

ManagePLUS Videos:
    www.goflagship.com/products/mpvideolib.htm

for QuickBooks

FormCalc for QuickBooks is an add-on that gives you calculated columns, column totals and subtotals, unique-item counts, and much more on your QuickBooks forms, such as Invoices, Sales Receipts, Estimates, and others—any form where Items are used.

Our customers use it for calculating shipping weights on invoices, box and pallet counts, area calculations on customer orders (yards of fabric, board-feet of lumber, etc.), quantity totals for meeting alcohol taxation record keeping requirements, and much, much more.

FormCalc works with most Microsoft Windows versions of Quick-Books, *including most older versions and most non-U.S. versions:* **US, UK, Canadian, and Australian!**

A **30-day free trial** is available to download—no commitment and no credit card required!

FormCalc on the Web:
  www.goflagship.com/products/fchome.htm

FormCalc Problem Solved™ examples:
  www.goflagship.com/products/fcprobsolved.htm

Catch Weights™ for QuickBooks

Catch Weights is an add-on for QuickBooks users in meat, seafood, and food wholesaling industries. It allows entering a list of catch weights—multiple individual weights—on any line of a QuickBooks Invoice or Sales Receipt, then writes the total weight in the Quantity column and adds the list of individual weights to the Description column.

Catch Weights works with most Microsoft Windows versions of QuickBooks, *including most older versions and most non-U.S. versions:* **US, UK, Canadian, and Australian!**

A **30-day free trial** is available to download—no commitment and no credit card required!

Catch Weights on the Web:
  www.goflagship.com/products/cwthome.htm

Catch Weights video:
  www.goflagship.com/products/cwthome.htm#video

The QuickBooks Farm Accounting Cookbook™

The QuickBooks Farm Accounting Cookbook™, by Mark Wilsdorf, is a

370-page book written for QuickBooks users in agriculture. This step-by-step guide and reference is written specifically for farmers and ranchers, and provides information about setting up QuickBooks for a farm business (Accounts, Classes, Lists, etc.) plus loads of transaction examples—all of them agricultural! It's called a "cookbook" because of its recipe-like approach to dealing with special agricultural accounting topics and problems.

The QuickBooks Farm Accounting Cookbook™ is another title in the **QuickBooks Cookbook**™ series from Flagship Technologies, Inc.

The QuickBooks Farm Accounting Cookbook™ on the Web:

    ⌨ www.goflagship.com/products/cbkhome.htm

Index

W

Made in the USA
San Bernardino, CA
01 October 2015